Is Multi-Level Marketing Right for You?

MLM

Is Multi-Level Marketing Right for You?

Hawkeye Richardson

2009

Table of Contents

PART 2: What to Do After Joining an MLM

PART 3: Final Thoughts

Introduction

MLM. Multi-level Marketing. Network marketing. Whatever you call it, MLM has established itself as a player in the marketplace. Millions of independent sales reps in the US (and around the world) promote and distribute products and services including cosmetics, jewelry, vitamin supplements, juices, clean water systems, legal and financial services, greetings cards, travel, timeshares, and many other products and services.

MLM companies range in size from brand new organizations that are just coming into the market, to companies which have sales in the billions of dollars. It is estimated that as many as one-in-every-fifteen people in the U.S. between the ages of 18 and 65 is involved or has been involved in an MLM company.

This means that you or someone you know may already be trying to 'make your fortune' at multi-level marketing. Whether you will be successful depends on a lot of factors, many of which may be out of your control.

Could you be one of the few people who make big bucks? Or are you more likely to be one of the millions of reps who lose money after expenses? This book will help you decide for yourself whether you 'have what it takes' to make it big.

Before I go any further, I want to clarify one key aspect of what I consider to be an MLM company, as opposed to 'direct sales.' In a direct sales company, you, as an independent rep, sell the company's product or service to consumers (and sometimes businesses). In direct sales, you make your money by selling the product/service and making a commission or getting a cut of the sales revenue.

As with any company selling a product or service, your earnings are based on how much product or service you sell on an on-going basis. Some people make a decent income selling in this way.

In an MLM company, you can make some money selling the product or service, but the **big** money is made by building 'teams' of reps under you, thus the term 'multi-level marketing'. Most of the estimated $100 billion in total sales in MLM companies is generated from 'recruiting' people onto 'teams' and selling them the product or service. Few sales are generated from the sale of the product or service to consumers who are not reps of the company.

In past times, the MLM industry was riddled with fraud and scams that came to be known as 'Pyramid Schemes'. In many of these companies, there were no actual products or services being provided. All the money was made by continuing to get the next person to sign under the next person, and so on.

Pyramid schemes are illegal in all 50 states. That doesn't mean they don't still exist. The recent news (2009) about Bernard Madoff and the money he defrauded from his investors was a good example of a complicated form of pyramid scheme.

As the Madoff example shows, identification, regulation, and enforcement of pyramid scheme problems are still inconsistent at best. Many of the MLM companies do the absolute minimum required to qualify as a legitimate business. Unfortunately, that legal minimum allows them to rip-off the 'average' participant. The reason these companies continue to get away with these practices is due to the fact that the initial investment is usually small. Most people won't take the MLM companies to court to get their money back when things don't work out as advertised.

The primary thing that multi-level marketing companies sell is 'Hope' --- hope that you, too, could leave your humdrum, boring, unsuccessful, financially-deficient life behind, and transform yourself into a multimillionaire in a matter of weeks or months.

Does every person have the possibility of becoming a millionaire in an MLM? --- Yes.

Is it easy? --- No.

Is it likely? -- No.

Will many people get to the millionaire status? --- No. Perhaps one rep in 10,000 might reach this level. And those who do will have specific characteristics that make it possible that they might be successful.

The primary purpose of this book is to help you cut through all the promotional hype and to give you a realistic view of Multi-Level Marketing and the chances that you can be successful at it.

Of course, this raises the question: *"What is the definition of Success?"* Only you can answer that question. For some people, earning an extra couple of hundred dollars a month would make them 'successful'. For others, 'success' means becoming a multi-millionaire.

Are either possible in MLM? --- Yes.

Will the 'average' person be 'millionaire' successful in an MLM business? -- No.

If you are considering getting into an MLM business (or have already done so), and if you expect to work only a couple of hours per week and become a millionaire in a year, you need to reset your expectations. There are some basic realities to being successful in any business, MLM or otherwise. To be really successful requires hard work, dedication, and, to be honest, a little bit of luck never hurts. But, this is true of almost any endeavor or business undertaking.

As you read the information that is presented in **Part 1: Things to Consider Before Joining an MLM**, use this information to determine whether and how you might become involved in an MLM business. Use it to set realistic goals, time parameters, and expectations.

If you are already in an MLM business but are not succeeding as well as you had hoped, **Part 2: What to Do After Joining an MLM** will offer you guidance on how to be more effective in your MLM business.

If you decide to join an MLM business, measure your success by your personal definition of success. Measuring your success against the Top 1% of people involved in an

MLM company is a sure way to crush your hopes and dreams. Big dreams require big efforts. Most people who become millionaires work 50-60 hour weeks for years before they build their businesses up to that level. An MLM business is no different.

Properly approached and managed, an MLM business can offer a number of different benefits. Unfortunately, for the average person, most of these benefits will not be related to making money.

If you are considering getting into an MLM business, I hope the information provided in this book will help you to make an honest and realistic assessment of the positive and negative aspects of MLM businesses, and your chances for success. If you are already in an MLM business, I hope this information helps you to be more successful.

PART 1:
Things to Consider Before Joining an MLM

Hawkeye Richardson

Chapter 1
Why do you want to become an Independent Rep in an MLM business?

There are many reasons why people get involved in an MLM business. Some join because they are bored and need something to do. Some join as a way to have social interaction with other people. Some join to learn about running their own business.

Of course, the majority join because they want to earn some money. A few want to earn an extra couple of hundred dollars a month to have as 'fun money'. Others need to generate a real income upon which to support a family. And then there are those who want to become multi-millionaires so that they don't have to work any more at all!

The first question for you to answer before joining an MLM is, why do you want to participate in an MLM business? (Check all that apply. If you check more than one, put a 'P' by the one which is the primary reason)

___ I will join purely for social reasons.

___ I will join because I am bored and need a hobby.

___ I want to join as a means of personal development.

___ I want to learn how to run my own business.

___ I want to earn a little extra fun money.

___ I need to earn a living through an MLM business.

___ I want to work hard to become wealthy through an MLM business.

If you are joining to eliminate boredom or for social reasons, find an MLM product/service you like, or a group of people in an MLM you like, and go for it. Since money isn't your primary concern, find an MLM that seems like it will be fun and which has fun people associated with it.

If you are considering joining an MLM as a way to make a little or a lot of money, that will require doing some research. It will also require doing an honest assessment of yourself to see if you 'have what it takes' to earn the amount of money you want or need to make from an MLM business.

That is what this book is designed to do -- to help you determine if you are one of the few who might make it big in an MLM; or whether you are one of the vast majority who will make little or nothing from an MLM investment.

Once you have indicated the reasons why you are considering joining an MLM, you are ready to proceed with Chapter 2.

Chapter 2
Joining an MLM for reasons other than making money

There are a number of reasons besides making money why a person might consider getting into an MLM business. In this chapter I want to discuss some of those reasons. Starting with Chapter 3, I will discuss how to determine if an MLM business might be right for you if you are primarily in it for the money.

Social Interaction

As human beings, most of us have an in-born need to interact with other people. While living in a cave as a hermit might sound attractive on occasion, most people need some interaction with other people to stay sane.

Many people get a good dose of their social interaction with other employees at their place of work. Unfortunately, many people are now self-employed (which is the essence of an MLM business). They work at home alone, or in a small office, with no other employees around with whom they can socialize, commiserate, complain and/or support each other.

If a person is single or is a person who craves more interaction than the narrowly-defined interactions he/she has with his/her immediate families and friends, it can be difficult to find a place or a group of people with similar interests with whom to spend time.

Getting involved in an MLM business can provide an opportunity to meet and interact with other people who, by definition, have at least one common interest -- the MLM business itself. In most MLM companies, there will be other local reps, up-line mentors, and down-line 'newbie's' who are involved in the business. They will often get together for training, recruiting, conventions, trips, and social events organized around the commonality of the group.

If you are planning to participate in an MLM primarily for social reasons, and if you plan to work at the business part-time, it is unlikely that you will make enough money from the business to break even after taking into account the expenses of being in the business.

Nevertheless, if the cost of being a rep isn't too high versus the benefits of the social interaction that are received, being a rep in an MLM could be an enjoyable, satisfying, and socially rewarding experience. You might consider the expenses of being in the business as one way to spend your monthly entertainment/fun money.

Once you have identified a couple of MLM businesses that interest you, attend some of their events, meetings, and perhaps even a convention, to see if the people who are involved in the business are people with whom you would enjoy socializing.

Of course, socializing with a group of fellow MLM'ers is no different than socializing with any other group.

There will always be some good apples and bad apples in the barrel. Concentrate on finding a group that welcomes you, that treats you with respect, and that feels good. Then, become an active member.

You are not in the group to be a wallflower, so get involved. As with many things in life, you tend to get out of something what you put into it. The sooner you proactively participate and socialize with members of the group, the sooner you may be accepted as a welcome addition.

Since you aren't getting into the MLM to make money, make sure the MLM group you pick isn't too over-focused on the business. Many MLM groups can be intense and business-focused. Try to find a group that also welcomes and accepts reps who aren't in it for the money, and a group that knows how to have fun outside of the business.

Learning to Run a Business

Many people have never had the opportunity (some might call it a curse) to run their own business. While colleges purport to teach people about business, the truth is, there is nothing like running your own business to get an education from the 'School of Hard Knocks.'

Anyone who thinks running your own business is easy has most likely never run their own business! There are many reasons why 50-70% of new small businesses don't survive their first year of operation: (1) under-capitalization, (2) inexperience, (3) competition, (4) over-confidence, and (5) a general lack of marketing and sales skills, would be some of the major reasons why the majority of new businesses don't last very long.

An MLM business can be an inexpensive way to dip-your-toe-in-the-water to see whether you are capable of paddling your own business canoe successfully. If you have never run your own business, starting with an MLM can be a great way to learn --- with one major caveat:

You would be well advised to have a separate and reliable source of income to live on while you learn how to run an MLM business successfully, (or any other type of business, for that matter.)

Like any other new business, an MLM business requires a full commitment of your time, your energy, your passion, and your resources.

Contrary to what is frequently 'advertised', the people who make decent money in an MLM business work at it fulltime. Forget the MLM marketing hype that says: "*Earn thousands of dollars a month working 10 hours a week.*" The only people who are making decent money in an MLM business and working 10 hours a week have been building their businesses for at least three, five, or maybe even ten years.

I don't know of any new business where a person can start from scratch and build a successful business working fewer than 40-60 hours a week for at least the first few years. An MLM business is no different.

MLM -- Is Multi-Level Marketing Right for You?

If you want to gain some experience in operating a business, and if you have a reliable source of income to live on while you learn, an MLM business can be an inexpensive and relatively safe way to learn some of the in's and out's of running a business --- without having to bet the farm.

One of the benefits of getting into an MLM business is that the MLM Company, itself, will have already invested a lot of money in marketing materials, sales training, branding, legal documents and contracts, and similar areas of setting up a business. On the positive side of the ledger, this saves the new MLM rep from having to develop these things him/herself. That's good.

On the other side of the ledger, however, is the fact that the rep has no voice or control over what goes into these materials. The MLM rep may also be restricted (sometimes severely) in how these materials can be used, in what ways, and in what forums.

In addition, while MLM companies may work to establish a 'brand' and an 'image', by definition, they rarely invest any money in local or national advertising on radio, TV, in magazines, or in any of the other forms of advertising that help build consumer awareness, confidence, and interest.

When you get right down to it, you -- the independent sales rep -- will be personally responsible for selling the product or service of the particular MLM Company you join. While you may get corporate training and materials to support you in your efforts, it is you who will ultimately have to put your proverbial 'feet-on-the-street' to make it happen.

In normal companies that have paid employees, this is called 'on-the-job-training.' The big difference is that with an MLM business, your independently-owned business, **YOU** are the boss, the employee, the salesperson, the accountant, the marketing director, the customer service rep, and the janitor, all rolled into one.

The point is, if you are going to become a business owner/manager, you might ask yourself the question: "*Is an <u>MLM</u> business the best way for me to learn what I want to learn about running a business?*"

If you have to rely on an MLM business to pay a decent living wage, <u>after expenses</u>, starting immediately, I would not recommend that a person join an MLM business. It takes most businesses a couple of years (maybe even five in today's economy) to develop to the point where the owner can make a good salary.

If you can't survive for at least a couple of years without making much net income from the MLM business, give serious consideration to getting a job with a regular company so that you have a steady stream of income to live on, and then dabble in an MLM business on the side.

Personal Growth and Development

Some people get into an MLM business as a way to develop their sense of self-worth, confidence, pride, and satisfaction, and as a way to define and expand their mental, emotional, and spiritual values. Many MLM companies offer 'personal development seminars' to their reps to help them become more confident and to develop a better sense and appreciation of their self-worth. Here, again, as long as you are not getting into an MLM business for the money, these self-development programs can be useful in helping you to find out who you are and what you want in life.

In my book "*Getting Your 'It' Together -- Simple Suggestions for Attracting the Life You Want*", I talk about how we live in a world that is dominated by the concept of **'MORE'** -- more money, bigger houses, faster cars. Unfortunately, much of the hype that surrounds many MLM companies focuses on "*becoming a millionaire overnight, earning free cars, free houses, glamorous vacations, and a new lifestyle that is worry free and full of wealth.*"

As you will learn in this book, few people ever attain these extravagantly high levels of income in an MLM business. Nevertheless, it is the hope of this wealthy lifestyle that attracts most people into an MLM.

Unfortunately, people who live their life always seeking MORE seldom ever get ENOUGH to satisfy themselves. Too many rich people are still unhappy, unfulfilled, and obsessed with chasing after 'just a little more'.

Part of running your own business is learning that building a successful business is hard work. Most business owners/managers learn (often after many years of chasing after more) that there are only a few really important things in life -- and having an obscene amount of money isn't necessarily one of them.

A close-knit family, good friends, good health, and an overall sense of well-being are worth more than all the money, cars and houses on the planet.

Did you know that over 50% of the people who won a major lottery between 1980 and 2000 were bankrupt within five years? So much for the belief that money alone can make us happy or solve life's problems.

Certain MLM businesses offer personal development seminars that can help you better define who you are and what you want in life. These programs may help you to have a better understanding of what would make you happy.

Nevertheless, there are also personal development programs offered by many companies that don't require you to join a business to gain access to the programs. If you are thinking of joining an MLM business primarily to take advantage of the personal development programs they offer, do some research first to see if there are other PD programs that would better suit your needs where you don't have to make an investment in a business to be able to participate in the program.

Chapter 3

What are the characteristics of a person who has the best chance to succeed in an MLM business?

Despite what the MLM companies say in their recruiting pitches, there are only certain types of people who are likely to have a chance at being successful in an MLM business. Are you one of those types of people? Answer the following questions to see if you 'have what it takes.' (Please answer the questions honestly if you want to get a true idea of whether you are likely to succeed at an MLM.)

1. Are you able to give yourself an honest evaluation of your skills, knowledge and experience as they relate to owning and managing a business?
    ___ Yes   ___ No

2. Do you consider yourself to be an extrovert?
    ___ Yes   ___ No

3. Do you have a separate source of income or savings upon which to live for two-to-five years while you are developing your MLM business?
    ___ Yes   ___ No

4. Would you feel comfortable and confident enough in yourself to tap someone on the shoulder in the grocery line -- a person you don't know -- to ask them if they are interested in travel, vitamins, jewelry, beauty products, or whichever MLM product/service you will be selling?
    ___ Yes   ___ No

5. Do you consider yourself to be a natural born salesperson? (Note: About seven percent of the population has the characteristics and personalities to be natural salespeople. Thus, the odds that you are one of those people are only 1 in 14.)
    ___ Yes   ___ No

6. Have you owned and operated a successful business before?
    ___ Yes   ___ No

7. Do you know lots of people and have lots of friends or contacts whom you would consider to be natural and successful salespeople?
    ___ Yes   ___ No

8. Can you put together a list of 500 people you would feel comfortable calling on the phone at their place of work to try to interest them in buying your MLM product/service?

      ___ Yes   ___ No

9. Will your personal ethics allow you to tell 'legal lies'* about a product or service to convince someone to buy it from you?

      ___ Yes   ___ No

10. Are you willing to work 50-60 hours a week for at least two-to-three years to build your business to the point where you can earn a decent salary to live on?

      ___ Yes   ___ No

(*Note: A couple of examples of 'legal lies' would be: "*Our product is totally unique and the absolute best in the marketplace;*" and, "*Everyone can make big money in an MLM business.*")

Okay, it's time for the moment of truth. Add up the number of questions to which you gave an answer of "*Yes*".

If you answered "*Yes*" to at least eight (8) of the questions, you have a <u>chance</u> at building a successful MLM business. That does not necessarily mean you are going to become rich. But, you at least have the characteristics of a person who has a chance to earn a decent living from an MLM business.

If you answered "*Yes*" to only six or seven questions, you might be able to earn some supplemental income from an MLM business. Nevertheless, it is unlikely that you will earn a full-scale salary that you can live on unless your monthly expenses are low.

If you answered "*Yes*" to fewer than six questions, you are likely to earn more money getting a part-time or full-time job at Wal-Mart or McDonalds than you will from being in an MLM business.

Now, I know there are some of you who are reading this who, after seeing the scores required to be successful, will want to go back and change some of your answers so that you qualify better than you did the first time.

My suggestion is -- "***Don't!***" If you know deep in your heart and soul that you don't have the necessary skills, personality, drive, confidence and commitment that are needed, don't lie to yourself. You will set yourself up for failure and disappointment, like the many people who got into an MLM 'hoping they, too, had what it takes.'

Based on the people I have met and looking at the people who seem to succeed best in an MLM business, three criteria standout as the most critical factors.

The first is that most of the big money earners were successful in other businesses before they got into an MLM. Of course, these people would naturally have a higher probability of succeeding at any new business, be it an MLM business or not. Success breeds success. And, the people who are successful tend to have many of the other characteristics which give them an advantage to being successful at any business.

The second key factor is that most of the successful people in MLM's are natural born salespeople. They could sell the proverbial 'refrigerator to an Eskimo.' What types of businesses and jobs do these people often have? Real estate; sales; people who are in jobs that generate lots of interaction with a lot of new people -- a hairdresser or a bartender, for example.

Then there are the celebrity types. By the mere fact that they have achieved celebrity status, they have already been successful in jobs such as acting, athletics, politics, senior business executives, or some other job with high visibility. Their celebrity status provides them with an 'implied trust' factor when they meet people (whether that trust is deserved or not.)

Thus, if you have a job with lots of visibility; if you have a job that provides lots of interaction with a continuously changing set of people; if you have been a successful business person; or if you have achieved some level of celebrity status, your odds of succeeding in an MLM are significantly increased.

For those of you who do not fit these categories, you may still be thinking (and hoping) that you are a person who can beat the odds. You believe you can be one of those people who reaches the Top 1%. If so, go for it! Don't let me get in the way of your dreams.

But, if you do decide to go for it, be prepared to give it your all, your best, your full and total commitment. If you go into it with less than a 100% commitment of effort and attitude, your chances of success are close to zero.

At this point, you might want to make a decision whether you still want to consider getting into an MLM business. If you need to make a decent living and if you don't fit the characteristics I have discussed, you may not need to go any farther in this book. Just admit that getting into an MLM business probably isn't a good idea, at least at this time.

Find a job, learn some additional skills, and gain more experience in some field in which you are interested. Trust me, MLM businesses, be they good or bad, are going to be around for a while. Thus, if at some future time you feel you are more prepared and want to give an MLM a go, there will still be MLM companies available to join.

Nevertheless, having said that, let me also say a couple more things. If you found that you don't fit the requirements to be successful in an MLM business, don't feel bad or feel like you are a failure. Remember, only seven percent of the population meets the characteristics of a natural born salesperson.

Also realize that government statistics show that, depending on the kind of business, <u>50%-70% of ALL new small businesses fail to survive through the first year of operation</u>; and only one of out ten will still be in business after ten years. Starting, owning and running any business is tough, even for people who have the skills and experience.

If you still feel that you want to pursue an MLM business, proceed to Chapter 4.

Chapter 4
Which MLM product or service do you <u>want</u> to sell?

If you are reading this chapter, it means you are still giving serious consideration to getting into an MLM business. That's great. The rest of the questions are designed to help you determine which, if any, MLM business would be best for you to join.

I am not going to discuss specific companies. Part of your 'education' in picking an MLM business involves studying the various companies and picking one that will best suit <u>your</u> needs. The material that follows is designed to help you find the MLM business that best suits your personality, your skills, and what you want to sell.

By the way, it is my recommendation that you investigate a number of different companies before selecting one to join. Furthermore, be proactive in deciding for yourself which one to consider.

<u>Don't be pressured into immediately joining the next 'hot company'.</u>

Remember, this is a business that you are looking to own and operate. Approach it logically, paying close attention to the REAL numbers and details, just as you would if you were buying a franchise, purchasing an existing business, or starting up a business from scratch on your own.

Don't be fooled or pressured by recruiting statements like: "*If you don't join today, the easy money will be taken by others.*" While it is true that the earlier you get into an MLM business, the better, the truth is that no matter when you get in, the odds are heavily stacked against your being able to make BIG money. I will address this specific issue in more depth in other chapters so let's move on for now.

The next question to ask yourself in your investigation is:

"Which MLM product or service do I want to sell?"

Which products or services fit your style and personality? Which products would you use personally so that you could give your own testimonials about their effectiveness?

If you do an online search for MLM products/services, you will find many different types and categories. There are products such as jewelry; health equipment; health supplements; vitamins; juices; beauty; travel; legal services; financial services; communications; entertainment. I'm not going to try to list them all here because there are too many and they are constantly changing anyway.

MLM -- Is Multi-Level Marketing Right for You?

Nevertheless, you need to look into what is available and determine what suits your fancy. Remember, you will have to continually sell this product or service or recruit a lot of people if you are going to make a decent income. Thus, it would be best to pick one that fits who you are.

It needs to be a product or service in which you can have confidence. You need to feel comfortable enough with the product or service that you could, in good conscience, sell it to your mother, your grandmother or your best friend. If you don't feel that you would be comfortable selling the product or service to people you care about, you are unlikely to feel comfortable selling it to strangers.

What I am saying is this: If you don't feel good about the product or service, you are unlikely to emit good, positive vibrations about it when you are trying to sell it. And, without a high level of confidence in what you are selling, you are unlikely to be successful on a long-term basis, even if you possess the qualities of a good salesperson.

So, it's time to do some homework. Think about which kinds of products or services you might be interested in selling. Which ones would you personally buy and use? Which ones would people you know be likely to buy and use on a long-term basis?

Get to a computer and go online and do some research. Identify the MLM companies that offer those types of products and narrow your search down to a half dozen on which you will do more detailed research.

Do online searches about the MLM industry (bring up Google on a computer that has Internet access, type in 'MLM', and hit <enter>). You'll find thousands of references related to MLM's. Read some of the articles that are available at various websites. Read articles that address both the positive and negative aspects of the MLM industry. The more you know about MLM companies, the better prepared you will be to determine which, if any, are best suited for accomplishing your goals.

And, please, do yourself a favor and don't buy any of the offerings from the hundreds of companies selling "*Automated MLM Sales Systems*" or "*The 13 Secrets to Success in an MLM Business.*" Finish reading this book before you invest any more of your money. If you want to purchase some of those systems later, you can. But, first, make sure that an MLM business is something you want to get into before you start spending much money.

List the MLM companies/products you think interest you the most. Then, proceed to Chapter 5.

Company #1: _____

Company #2: _____

Company #3: _____

Company #4: _____

Company #5: _____

Company #6: _____

Chapter 5
What is the unique need that the MLM product or service satisfies that is not already being offered in the marketplace?

If you are considering joining an MLM, the question you should consider next is: "*What need does this product or service satisfy that isn't already being met by an existing product or service?*"

Hey, it's a big world out there. You are going to have to sell your product in a world where there are millions of companies that offer products and services. Those companies may be local, regional, national or international.

With the advent of the Internet, you can purchase a pair of socks from China as easily as you can from the local Wal-Mart (of course, the socks sold at Wal-Mart were made in China!)

The question is, what is unique about the product or service you will sell in your MLM business that gives you a selling advantage over any other company offering a similar product? If it doesn't have something unique about it, it will be much harder to sell on a long-term basis.

Is it cheaper? Faster? Bigger? Louder? Easier to use? Come in more colors?

Is it the latest, greatest and hottest? Will it last longer? Does it come with a better or longer guarantee? Can your customers get their money back if they don't like it?

Can you deliver the product or service faster to your clients? Are you more conveniently located to your customers? Will the product be fresher because you are closer to them?

Does it have some secret ingredient that makes it special?

Please recognize that no special ingredient stays secret for long. Every new health juice or supplement touts "*the secret ingredient that is only grown by 100 year-old gurus in the back of their monastery in the remote foothills of Bamboozle-land.*"

This is just marketing hype. The problem with secret ingredients is that they will not be exclusive in the marketplace for long. Whether it is an Acai Berry, a Goji Berry, or *eye of newt, powdered bat tongue, or fricasseed Hummingbird knees*, its exclusivity will be short-lived. Usually, it will last just long enough for the Top 1% of the MLM company reps to make the big bucks and move on leaving you with --- what?

If you plan to make a living selling an MLM product or service, select one that has natural longevity to it. Select something that people will consume on an on-going basis, not some fad that will come and go in a matter of months.

What types of products and services have a longer lifespan? A quick look will show that makeup, and companies that sell a broad variety of consumable household products have more proven longevity. Those companies that offer only one product or service are much less likely to provide repeat sales over the long haul.

If you want to make a living from an MLM business over a longer time period, you will have a higher likelihood of success going with a company that offers a wide array of products. With a wider variety of products, you have a better chance of finding at least one product that people need and will continue to use.

Chapter 6
Who is the target market for the product or service and how many of them are there?

Every business has to identify its target market. An MLM business is no different. Unfortunately, if you listen to the *"numbers of people who need/want this service"* as touted, shouted, and spouted by the MLM recruiters, you are led to believe that everyone and his/her sister, brother, father, mother, aunt, uncle, friend, co-worker, spouse, in-law, neighbor, Baby Boomer, Generation X'er, any person who is still breathing, and, perhaps, even a few pets, have a significant, unfulfilled need for the particular product or service!

Unfortunately, such is not the case. Think about it for a moment. Can you think of a single product or service that (1) you want, (2) that you can afford, (3) that you don't already have, (4) where you don't know a store or company that offers the product or service? If you are like most people, if there is a product or service that you want and can afford to buy, you know a place to get it.

An MLM business is just another provider of products and services. When you sell your product directly to consumers, yours is just one more they have to choose from.

Even though this might seem to be contrary to what you might believe, the more narrowly you can define the target market group, the more likely you are to succeed. Let me give an example: Baby Boomers.

Baby Boomers are all the people in the United States who were born from 1946-1964. (The Baby Boom started at the end of World War II and came to an end in 1964, the year the birth control pill became widely available.)

As of July 1, 2005, there were an estimated 78,200,000 Baby Boomers still alive in the U.S. These people started reaching retirement age (62) in 2008. Supposedly, 10,000 boomers will retire each day for the next 30 years.

Man! That sounds like a huge market doesn't it? And, it is. Nevertheless, not all 78 million Boomers will buy the same product.

An example of one of the big markets the Boomers are supposed to create is an exploding travel industry. The MLM recruiters are quick to point out: "*What do people want to do when they retire? -- TRAVEL!*"

Well, yes, and no. Will some BB's want to travel more after they retire? Yes. But, that doesn't mean that they didn't travel <u>before </u>they retired. In addition, because of the recent recession and many businesses going bankrupt and eliminating pension plans, many Boomers find that the money they had saved for their retirement isn't going to go as far or last as long as they had hoped.

Many Boomers are delaying retirement and many are having to go back to work to earn enough to live on.

MLM -- Is Multi-Level Marketing Right for You?

Many Boomers have gotten bored of being retired and have gone back to work to keep from going stir crazy.

Thus, while Baby Boomers represent a large potential market, that does not mean they are all potential prospects for what you are selling.

Another key differentiator is --- gender. Men and women represent significantly different markets. How many men do you know who purchase products from Avon, Arbonne or Mary Kay? Darn few, I'll bet.

Even among women, women of age 25 versus 45 versus 65 do <u>not</u> have the same needs.

Before you decide which MLM company to join, do some research to find out who the target market is for the product or service that will be offered. Once you have identified this target group, ask yourself how many people you know who fit that target group. Those are the people you will have to sell to if you are to be successful.

One piece of information that would be useful to know is, how many potential customers are there for this product or service in your area? While many MLM companies will talk about how you can develop recruits and markets anywhere, even abroad, the truth is that most of your sales will be generated locally. Don't count on developing a team in Mexico, Canada or the Middle East as a quick and easy way to make big bucks.

How does one try to estimate the size of the market for a given product or service? While it's not easy, you can make some educated guesses by doing research on the Internet. Let me give an example.

Let's assume that you are considering joining an MLM that sells vitamin supplements, either in tablet or juice form. Let's suppose you live in the city of Anywhere,

USA. It has a population of 100,000 people. According to surveys that I found online, it is estimated that <u>50% of adults in the U.S. take vitamin supplements but only half of those take the vitamins daily</u>.

Subtracting 20% of the population of Anywhere which represents children under the age of 13 (they are not 'adults' so we have to subtract them from the total population of 100,000), and subtracting 50% of the adults based on the survey data, this leaves a total vitamin-taking population of adults and older children in Anywhere of approximately 40,000 people.

Let's further assume that these vitamin-takers spend an average of $25 per month on vitamins. There is, therefore, a total potential for sales of vitamins of $12,000,000 per year (40,000 people times $25 of vitamins per month times 12 months equals $12 million dollars of total vitamin sales).

$12,000,000 will be spent on vitamins in Anywhere during the year. But, where are those 40,000 vitamin-takers going to buy those vitamins? The answer is --- lots of places. They can conveniently buy them at the grocery store, at the drugstore, and at specialty stores in strip malls and shopping centers.

According to a recent survey, drug stores control over 44 percent of the vitamin market. Grocery stores account for another 30 percent. Specialty stores that sell vitamins in strip malls and shopping centers account for another 15%. And Internet sales account for an estimated 6%. That adds up to a total of 95% of all vitamin purchases being made in these four types of stores.

Therefore, only 5% of total sales of vitamins are left to be filled through all other types of businesses, including sales through MLM businesses.

In Anywhere, that leaves $600,000 worth of vitamin sales to be made by MLM companies and others. Now, please note that this is $600,000 of gross sales, before expenses. It is not the commissions that will be made on the sales.

Let's assume that the MLM vitamin product you are selling pays you a 50% commission (which is a high figure. The average MLM commission on a product sale is closer to 20%). Anyway, using this 50% commission figure means that there is approximately $300,000 worth of potential commissions to be made selling MLM vitamin products in Anywhere.

The next question to ask is, how many different MLM company reps are already operating in Anywhere selling vitamin supplements? A quick glance at any listing of MLM companies shows dozens of different companies selling vitamin supplements in either tablet or juice form. Let's assume there are 10 different MLM companies represented by reps in Anywhere. Let's further assume that each company has 10 reps selling in the Anywhere marketplace.

Ten companies with ten reps each equals 100 total reps. Dividing the $300,000 of potential commissions by 100 reps equals an average ANNUAL commission of $3,000 per year, per rep!

In truth, 90% of the reps won't make a dime. And, even for those that do make a commission, that is an average of $3,000 per year, **before expenses**.

Hawkeye Richardson

Do these numbers represent an accurate estimate of the potential commissions that an average rep might make in any given marketplace selling vitamins? That depends on the population of the market, the number of MLM Companies currently serving the market, and the number of reps in those companies.

But, let's suppose for a moment that those numbers are accurate. Would you want to start a new MLM business selling vitamins to strangers in this town of Anywhere, USA? I wouldn't.

The point of this discussion is that spending some time doing research on the Internet can give you at least a ballpark estimate of the potential sales and commissions that you might make selling the product or service in your local area. And, it is further evidence that the big money made in MLM's is not made by selling the product. The big money is made by recruiting more reps who will, unfortunately, end up earning even less money.

- 38 -

Chapter 7
What is the price and frequency of purchase of the product or service?

Two of the factors that will impact how much you make in your MLM business are the price of the MLM product or service you will be selling and how often the customer buys it.

I teach a two-hour class on advertising at a local organization that helps new small businesses to get started. One of the questions that I always ask at the start of the class is: "*How much is your average customer sale likely to be?*"

I'm always fascinated that fewer than one out of ten of the 'soon-to-be-new-business-owners' can answer this simple question. When you stop and think about it, the answer to this simple question is a critical component, not just in advertising the business, but in determining how many customers the business will need to generate the sales (and profit/salary) desired by the owner.

Suppose you decide that you want to earn $30,000/yr. (net after taxes and expenses) from your MLM business. Suppose also that you have an income tax rate of 18%

and that the commission on the product you will sell is 50%. Dividing $30,000 by 82% (100% - 18% = 82%) equals $36,585. Thus, you must earn $36,585 of commissions to net $30,000 after taxes. (Please note that this does not take into account the expenses you will incur in the business, an issue I address in Chapter 9)

With a net margin of 50%, you will have to generate $73,170 of gross sales to generate $36,585 of commissions ($36,585 / 50% = $73,170).

The question to ask next is, how many customer sales do you have to close to generate $73,000 worth of gross sales?

If you sell a product that will generate average annual sales per customer of $500, you will have to convince 146 prospects to buy your product. Is that doable? Maybe. (Note: If you sell a product that costs the customer $42 every month, this will generate annual sales of approximately $500).

If you are selling vitamins, this might be a tough sell. If you are selling fancy cruises, it might not be too hard.

Regardless of whether it will be easy or hard to make a sale, the fact is you will have to make about three sales a week to meet your goals (3 sales/week * 52 weeks = 156 total sales, a few more than the 146 that are needed). Thus, when you are planning your advertising, marketing and appointment schedules, you will need to talk to enough people to generate three sales, week-in and week-out for a whole year.

If you are able to convert one out of four sales pitches into a paying customer (a phenomenal rate that you are unlikely to achieve), you would have to identify, schedule, and present to at least 584 prospects a year (146

* 4 = 584). With 250 work days per year (excluding weekends) you will have to schedule and present to a little more than two appointments every day to meet your goals.

But, you will have to make a lot more than 584 phone calls to get 584 appointments scheduled. If you are able to schedule one presentation out of every ten phone calls you make (which would be better than average over time for salespeople in an MLM business today), you will need to make at least 5,840 phone calls a year to schedule enough presentations to meet your needs. With 250 work days, you will have to make at least 23 calls per day, or about 3 every hour to meet your goals.

Wow! That's a bunch! And, your initial list of 500 'warm leads' includes a lot of people who (1) have no need for your product, (2) who are on the Do Not Call list (thus, even if you call them they won't want to talk to you, so why bother), and (3) who have already been approached or participated in an MLM business (most -- unsuccessfully).

Are you starting to get the picture that this business requires a lot of work and time? The marketing hype about working only 2 hours a week is just that -- baloney! To make a <u>living</u> at an MLM business, you will probably end up working 50-60 hours per week, at least for the first couple of years, just like you would if you started any other kind of small business.

But, before you decide whether this MLM stuff is for you, let's look at two more examples based on a different average sale per customer.

Suppose you sell a product that generates an average sale per customer of only $250 per year? The math is simple. You will have to double the number of sales presentations to earn your $30,000. You will have to make four presentations every working day of the year in order to close 292 sales (146 * 2 = 292). (292 * $250 = $73,000.)

To accomplish that, you will have to make 1,168 presentations (292 *4 = 1,168). To schedule that many presentations, you will have to make approximately 11,680 phone calls; about 47 phone calls per day; roughly six every hour; one every ten minutes.

Whew! I'm getting tired just thinking about this.

Let's look at one more example. But, this time, let's factor in some 'recruiting' bonuses and commissions from your team's sales in addition to your commissions on straight product sales.

Let's assume that the average customer sale is $1,000. If you can sell 40 people, how much will you have to make in recruiting bonuses and sales by people under you to reach your $30,000 income goal?

Let's assume that you get 3% of your team's first year sales volume as another bonus.

The 40 customers you personally sold would produce total sales of $40,000. You get 50% of that as commission so you earned $20,000 toward your $30,000 goal! Good job!

Okay, so far you have made $20,000 towards your $30,000 goal. Of the 40 people you recruited, let's assume that 10 of them also joined to get into the MLM business to recruit their own teams (as opposed to just using the product or service.) For each of those 10 recruits, you get a $250 bonus from the company. Thus, you earned another $2,500 in bonuses.

MLM -- Is Multi-Level Marketing Right for You?

Finally, let's assume that the 10 new recruits you signed in the first year also sold 40 customers who generated average annual sales of $1,000. Thus, total sales from your team would equal $400,000 (400 * $1,000 = $400,000).

Assuming that you get 3% of your team's volume, you would earn an additional $12,000 from their sales (3% * $400,000 = $12,000).

If we add up everything you earned through the year, you would have earned a total of $34,500 ($20,000 in sales commissions, $2,500 of recruitment bonuses, and $12,000 of sales commissions from your team's sales.)

Well, congratulations! You <u>almost</u> met your goal. (This example didn't factor in taxes or expenses, thus you will have to sell even more to reach your goal of $30,000 <u>after</u> taxes and expenses. The issue of expenses in your MLM business is addressed in Chapter 9.)

If you think that you could have made that many phone calls, closed that percentage of your calls, and helped recruit team members who could accomplish the same productivity, you might be able to make this MLM business successful enough to earn the living you needed.

Obviously, the numbers for Year 2 start to build on your first year's numbers. You will receive sales commissions on your own customer's purchases next year, a percentage of your team's sales, plus the new sales and bonuses you will earn by adding more new customers in Year 2.

But, you also have to take into account that many of the 440 new customers from last year (40 of your own and 40 each from the customers your 10 team members each sold) will not renew for another year. It is not unusual to see 25%-75% of customers drop off after the end of the first year. Why?

Many customers will find the product or service wasn't as good as advertised. Many will move on to the next 'fad' product that promises "*a cure for all that ails them.*" Many will grow tired of seeing that $83 going out every month ($1,000 / 12 = $83 per month.)

And, many of those 10 people you recruited who wanted to build their own teams will be disappointed that they didn't make the million dollar level in their first year as expected -- and they, too, will quit.

Assuming that 50% of your customers quit by the end of the first year, you would start Year 2 with 20 of your own customers and only 220 of your teams' customers.

Putting that all together, you might start Year 2 with 'residual sales commissions' to be generated from existing customers of perhaps $16,000 -- $10,000 from your remaining 20 customers, plus $6,000 from the remaining 200 customers your team sold (200 * $1,000 * .03% = $6,000).

As you can see, if you stay in this MLM business long enough and if you can keep a fair percentage of your customers and the customers your team sells, eventually, you could make some decent money.

But, before you get too excited and head for the bank, remember that in this example you were selling a product or service that costs the customer $1,000 a year. These people are harder to find and to sell to than a customer who could afford $250 or $500 a year. Thus, you might have to make 20 calls to get an appointment, and you might close only one out of ten presentations. Thus, to generate your 40 sales, you might have to make 8,000 phone calls, or 32 calls a day; four every hour. And, the recruits under you will have to do the same.

As you can see, the number of phone calls, presentations, recruiting duties, support of your team, and so forth, can get large, pretty fast. When it all works, you could make some decent money.

The purpose of this Chapter was to help you see the relationship between the average annual sales price of the product or service you plan to sell, the frequency of purchase, and how many customer sales you will have to close during the year. Plus, the team members you recruit will have to duplicate your numbers.

I want to end this chapter by mentioning one other concern that you should consider.

If you are having trouble understanding a lot of these calculations and numbers, you probably shouldn't run your own business. The calculations you have seen and the examples given are simple compared to some of the complex Compensation Plans discussed in Chapter 16. The more complex the Comp Plan, the harder it is to figure out how many customers you will need to sell, and the harder it is to figure out if the MLM company is paying you what you are owed.

If you are having trouble with all these numbers, please give serious thought as to whether you should own and operate your own business. You might be better off getting a job at someone else's company where they take the risks and handle the numbers.

Chapter 8
Can you afford the
initial investment?

The good news about most MLM companies is that the initial investment needed to get started in the business is relatively low. Initial investments of $250 - $5,000 are common. This is a much lower amount than is generally needed to start many other types of businesses.

Nevertheless, the questions you must ask yourself are: "*Do I have the money for the initial investment and for the on-going expenses of the business, until it starts self-funding itself through product/service sales and recruiting bonuses?*"

I will address the on-going expenses of an MLM business in Chapter 9. For now, we are interested only in the initial investment.

For people who are getting into an MLM as a hobby or as a way to socialize, the money might not be an issue. Since money is not the reason these people are thinking of joining an MLM, and if they can afford the investment, then they might think of the initial investment as an investment in fun or entertainment.

Nevertheless, for those people who are getting into an MLM specifically to make money, there are generally two categories that people fall into:

> Group 1: They have some money in savings or a job, and they are looking to supplement their income with earnings from an MLM.

> Group 2: They have little money, little savings, no job, and need to find a way to start making some money fast as a way to pay the bills.

If you are thinking of joining an MLM as a way to earn money, which of these two types of people more closely defines your current situation? If you are a person in Group 1, then you can decide how much you have available and how much you are willing to invest to get into an MLM business.

If, on the other hand, you are in Group 2, you might have a bigger problem on your hands. That problem is, even if you have the money for the initial investment, you need to understand that it takes a lot of time for the 'average' person to start making a meaningful amount of money from an MLM business.

If you need to earn $2,500 a month to pay for living expenses, it is likely to take many months or even years to reach that level in an MLM business.

Regardless of what the MLM recruiters say, <u>making serious money in an MLM business does not happen quickly</u>. From that standpoint, it is no different from starting any other kind of business. It is not unusual for a new, small business to take three years before it reaches breakeven where the owner/manager can take a real salary.

So, if you are desperately in need of a significant salary, you would probably be better off looking for a job with an existing company.

While you might make a few quick bucks in the first couple of weeks in an MLM business from sympathy sales from people on your 'warm leads list' (family and friends), once that list is exhausted (which is likely to happen in the first month or two), you will have to start cold calling just like everyone else. And, in today's world, it isn't easy to find a cost-effective way to cold call consumers, especially with the advent of the Do Not Call Registry.

As unappealing as it might sound, if you need to start making a real salary immediately, you would probably be better off spending your time sending out resumes and getting job interviews, because making real money from an MLM won't happen overnight.

This brings us back to the original investment. If you are still thinking of getting into an MLM, how are you going to fund the initial investment? Do you have enough in savings to pay for it? Are you going to charge it to a credit card? Can you afford to make the payments on the credit card while you are getting the business up and going?

Can you borrow the money for the initial investment from family or friends? Can you borrow money from your IRA or an insurance policy? Regardless of how you fund the initial investment, be aware that there are going to be additional expenses beyond the initial investment that will have to be funded. For an idea of what the on-going expenses could be, read on in Chapter 9.

Chapter 9
What are the expenses you might incur in your MLM business?

In Chapter 7 I talked about the level of gross sales you might have to achieve, under certain assumptions, to be able to earn a net income of $30,000 after taxes. Unfortunately, those calculations did not include the expenses associated with operating your own MLM business.

"*But,*" you say, "*I get to deduct my expenses off my income taxes before calculating what I owe. That will make a big difference, won't it?*"

The answer is "*Yes*" and "*No.*"

<u>(DISCLAIMER: Sorry, but if I don't put this information here, some of you will fail to seek the guidance of a tax professional and then you will be mad at me when things didn't turn out the way you hoped. So, please note that it is not the purpose of this book to help you calculate the impact of an MLM business on your income tax returns. You need to seek the help of a qualified tax professional</u>

before you decide what expenses you might be able to legally deduct against the income of your business and other income you might have. The author and publisher accept no responsibility or liability from your use or misuse of the information contained in this book, nor any responsibility or liability for any taxes, fines or other consequences of actions you might take relative to things discussed in this book.)

Having said that, yes, it is likely that you will get to deduct at least <u>some</u> of your MLM business expenses against your income before calculating the taxes you owe. Which expenses you can deduct vary by the kind of business, what kind of company you have setup in which to operate your MLM business (LLC, Sole Proprietor, and other forms), and other factors. <u>The following examples are given only to discuss some of the types of expenses you might incur in running your business, not which ones are legally deductible.</u>

There are many expense items that are associated with operating almost any business. The purpose of this chapter is to make you aware of the expense side of running an MLM business and the impact it can have on your ability to earn the money you need.

In virtually any business, there are expenses associated with operating it. In an MLM business, you might or might not choose to deduct (or be able to deduct) expenses related to an office or a store. Since most MLM businesses are run from people's homes, the usual expenses related to 'facilities' might not apply.

The first expense of an MLM business is the initial investment. Depending on how you set up the company and the amount of money involved, you might be able to take this full expense in Year 1, or you might have to amortize that expense over a number of years. Based on the amount you expect to invest in the particular MLM you are considering, ask your Tax Consultant how much of this expense you will be able to 'write off' in the first year.

The amount of the initial investment is important. To buy a franchise such as a hamburger joint or even an ice cream stand, the initial investment could be tens of thousands of dollars, or much more. One of the reasons why many people choose to have an MLM business is that the initial investment is low, both in terms of the initial amount paid to the MLM Company, and the money required for things such as sales materials, inventory, and so forth.

The initial investment in most MLM companies will range between $250 - $5,000 depending on the product, the Compensation Plan, and whether the rep must invest in inventory for sales or demonstration purposes. Recognize that this is only the initial investment. It does not include many other potential expenses.

What are some of those expenses? Those expenses might include some/all/none of the following:

1. Sales Materials: (Brochures, magazines, CD's, DVD's, signup forms, Disclosure Statements, product samples, product inventory for display)
2. Training materials, CD's, DVD's.
3. Phone expenses (Cell Phone, Land Line, Internet Connection fees)
4. Office supplies

5. Travel expenses (around town for car gas and maintenance; trips to company conventions, events, and training seminars; meals; hotel rooms, rental cars, airfare, tips)

6. Expenses related to putting on public recruiting events (hotel or restaurant room fees; equipment; name tags and signs; refreshments for Visitors/Prospects/Reps ;)

7. Expenses related to doing 'Home Parties' (Refreshments, name tags, equipment, tables, signs)

8. Expenses for equipment for registering new customers online and for online training, education, and website usage (computer, software, printer, projector, screen, internet hookup, speakers, microphones)

9. Meals associated with attending local recruiting events

10. 'Home office' furniture and equipment, desks, tables, chairs.

11. 'Home office' utilities (electricity, gas)

12. Insurance (Liability, business inventory, theft, and so forth)

13. Monthly/Annual fees for maintaining your membership in an MLM company;

14. Expenses related to advertising and marketing (website design, hosting, print ad design and placement, electronic sales, i.e. Google Adsense, Yahoo, Amazon.com ads.)

15. Annual dues/fees/memberships in business and networking organizations such as a

Chamber of Commerce, networking clubs, community groups such as Rotary, and small business associations. Plus, expenses for breakfasts, lunches and 'mixers'.

As you can see, running an MLM business may not be that different from running any other kind of small business. One major difference, however, is that you probably won't have any employees (and all the expenses and hassles that come with them).

You might not have any office expense if you run the business out of your home and if you choose not to go through the hassle of providing the IRS with the necessary info to justify the home office expense.

(Also, please note that most homeowners' insurance policies usually do not cover business inventory stored in the home or in your car; equipment; liabilities associated with running the business; nor theft of business property. Thus, if you are planning to operate your business out of your home, you should check with your insurance agent to see if you need additional insurance to cover the business.)

A cell phone to handle your calls both in the office and while out and about might cost you $100 per month. Internet access fees can add another $25 - $50. Business cards cost $50-$100 for 500.

If you live in a city, you can easily drive 30-50 miles a day getting to various events and appointments. That can add up to 7,500 - 12,500 miles a year. The IRS mileage deduction is around 50+ cents per mile so you can figure your expenses to be about the same. That means you might incur actual auto expenses (gas, maintenance, insurance, registration & license fees) of approximately $3,750 - $6,250 a year, or an average of $300 - $525 per month. (Yes, you will probably get to write off some of that mileage. But, it is still money out of your pocket.)

You could easily spend $50-$500/month on sales materials and product samples.

There is likely to be a monthly or annual fee to pay the MLM Company for your continuing membership, or for maintaining your company website. This could range from $25 - $100 per month or more.

If you join a couple of business organizations as a way to meet potential customers, and as a way to find 'recruits' and sell your products/services, annual dues could be $150 - $500. Bi-monthly/weekly meetings (breakfasts and lunches) and 'mixers' where people meet somewhere after work to have drinks and network, can easily add $100 - $200 to your monthly expenses.

When you start to add up these expenses, you might find that you have on-going monthly expenses of $1,000-$2,000 a month or more.

If you go to a company convention during the year (which will often be out of your area), you can have the registration fee for attending the convention ($250 - $500), plus airfare and rental car expenses if you can't drive to the convention.

Then you have hotel room expenses that will average $100 - $200 per night (these conventions are usually held in big cities where prices are higher).

Plus meals. Plus tips. Plus souvenirs.

Add this all up and you might find your annual business expenses for owning and operating an MLM business to be $10,000 - $50,000 per year.

MLM -- Is Multi-Level Marketing Right for You?

Now, while you will get to deduct <u>some</u> of these expenses for tax purposes, let's make sure you understand what that means and the impact it might have on your net income.

As we all know, the government makes it complicated and confusing to figure out one's taxes. There are many variables and types of deductions, variances by state, variances based on the level of income ($15,000 gets taxed at a different rate than $75,000), etc. Because of all these variations, it would be impossible for me to tell you how to calculate your exact income, expenses, income taxes, and everything else that is associated with running your own MLM business.

Nevertheless, I want to give you a simple example of an independent rep who owns an MLM business and show you how the gross sales, commission rate, expenses, and taxes impact the volume of sales necessary for this rep to make $30,000 a year.

Remember, the purpose of this example is to give you an idea of the expenses associated with an MLM business and the impact it will have on the income you wish to make. It does not represent an actual calculation of income and expenses that you might receive or incur.

For purposes of this example, let's assume we have a person named Charlie. Charlie is single, aged 30, with no children or other dependents. Charlie is an independent rep for the "Whoop-Ti-Do" MLM company. Whoop-Ti-Do manufactures and sells vitamin supplements through its independent reps. Charlie established his MLM business as a Limited Liability Corporation (LLC), which gives him some liability protection against his personal assets.

Charlie has been selling Whoop-Ti-Do products for a couple of years. At the end of last year, Charlie figured his gross sales with the company to be $125,000. Charlie has a 50% commission rate. Thus, he received $62,500 in total commissions from the company.

With his tax professional's assistance, Charlie calculated that he had $20,000 of **deductible** expenses during the year. Thus, on his income taxes, Charlie deducted $20,000 off of his gross income of $62,500 before he calculated the rest of his taxes. Charlie ends up with an Adjusted Gross Income of $42,500.

(Please note that the $20,000 in deductible expenses might not represent all of Charlie's expenses, and those expenses represent $20,000 that he has already paid out of his pocket to run the business, whether he generated any sales or not.)

Since Charlie is self-employed (an LLC passes through income to Charlie's household for tax purposes in the same manner as if Charlie were a sole proprietor), he will have to pay Self-employment Social Security taxes and Medicare Taxes on his Adjusted Gross Income. For the tax year of 2009, as a self-employed person, Charlie calculates his Social Security and Medicare Taxes based on 92.35% of his Adjusted Gross Income. That equals $39,248. ($42,500 * .9235 = $39,248.)

Charlie next takes the combined Social Security plus Medicare tax rate of 15.3% times the $39,248 of income. This equals $6,005. That is the amount of SS and Medicare taxes Charlie will have to send in along with his income taxes.

Charlie gets to deduct half of the $6,005 from his Adjusted Gross Income before he calculates his income taxes. Thus, he gets to subtract $3,002 dollars from the $42,500 which equals $39,498.

As a single person, Charlie has opted to take the standard deduction for his household which is equal to 12.3% of his adjusted income. This equals $4,858.

Charlie also gets to take one 'personal exemption' of $3,500.

He ends up with Net Adjusted Income of $34,142. ($42,500 - $4,858 - $3,500 = $34,142.)

When Charlie looks up $34,142 in the Federal Income Tax Tables, he finds that he owes the Federal government $5,190 of income taxes.

Finally, Charlie lives in Arizona where he will pay an amount equal to 21% of his Federal Income tax amount to the state for income taxes. This equals $1,090 ($5,190 * .21 = $1,090.)

Thus, out of the $62,500 that Charlie was paid in commissions, he had $20,000 of out of pocket expenses leaving him with $42,500.

From that he will pay out $6,005 of Social Security and Medicare taxes, $5,190 of Federal Income taxes and $1,090 of State Income taxes.

Therefore, out of the $125,000 of gross sales that Charlie sold, he will end up with $30,215 of net income after taxes and expenses!

Wahoo! If Charlie wanted to make at least $30,000 from his MLM business, he achieved his goal!

At $500 per average customer sale, Charlie has to close the sale on 250 customers to generate $125,000 of gross sales. That is the equivalent of one customer every business day of the year.

At $250 for an average annual customer sale, Charlie would need 500 average customer sales for the year, or an average of 10 per week.

One of the problems in generating enough sales to provide a decent salary for the year is that you will <u>have</u> to spend money on various forms of marketing or advertising (recognize that <u>YOU</u> are the advertisement at a business group luncheon, but you still have the expense of the group's annual dues and the cost of meals at the meetings, plus mileage going to the meetings).

You will most likely need to spend money on sales materials and/or product samples. You will have to have a computer, a phone, and office supplies. To get the level of training you need to be successful you will need to attend training seminars and some of the company events. In Charlie's' example (which might represent an average amount of expenses to generate $125,000 sales in an MLM), he had $20,000 worth of expenses.

As another example, a rough rule of thumb in business is to spend about 10% of gross sales on advertising. Thus, to achieve $125,000 of sales, one would expect to spend about $12,500 just on <u>advertising</u> related activities.

Then there are the other expenses that exist in almost every business: Phone bills, travel, memberships, training, office supplies, equipment, etc. Thus, ending up with $20,000 of expenses in an MLM business that generates $125,000 of sales would be normal, maybe low.

MLM -- Is Multi-Level Marketing Right for You?

(Please note that in a regular business, you might also have an expense called "Cost of Goods Sold." In our example, this expense is paid by the MLM Company from the 50% that it takes as its share of gross sales.)

There are two major points to take from this discussion: First, when the MLM companies state that you will have minimal expenses and still be able to make the big bucks, it just isn't true. An MLM business has expenses just like any business would incur. If you want to generate a given level of sales, you will have to advertise, market, travel, get training, setup appointments, attend meetings, and make sales presentations. And, the truth is, all those things cost money.

The second thing to take from this discussion is that running a business requires working with a lot of numbers: tracking, tabulating and calculating expenses; calculating and paying taxes; tracking, calculating and collecting commissions.

If you are uncomfortable dealing with all these numbers, perhaps owning and managing your own business, an MLM business or otherwise, is not for you. But, only you can make that decision.

I have tried to show you some of the things that are involved in running an MLM business and making a decent salary. In truth, it is a full-time job. For most small business owners, that can mean 50-60 hours of work per week and it might take 3-5 years before the company is generating a solid profit and a good salary for the owner.

Chapter 10
What kinds of sales and marketing support are available?

As has been noted in some of the previous chapters, you will be the primary (as in -- only) salesperson for your independent MLM business. One of the benefits of joining an MLM is that the MLM Company will have already prepared sales and marketing materials to help you do your job. This can be a significant advantage versus having to design and produce all these materials yourself.

Having said that, the availability of these materials does not solve the major problem of marketing your product or service. The first big hurdle is to get yourself in front of the prospect. In truth, only then will the sales and marketing materials be of any use.

The impact of the recession is forcing many companies to look for more cost-effective ways to market to their customers and prospects. Unfortunately, the options for advertising a business are limited and often expensive. And, **with an MLM business, you might be prohib-**

ited from using one or more of these normal methods of advertising.

- Print ads in newspapers/magazines <u>are expensive and targeted only by geography.</u>
- Radio and TV ads can be expensive, have no extended life to them (once the ad runs, it's gone), and <u>are targeted and delivered only at a broad geographical level or by program type</u>.
- Direct mail can be expensive and people are inundated with advertising pieces in their mail box. Putting together a successful direct mail campaign is both an art and a science that the average business owner cannot effectively accomplish on his/her own. In addition, many MLM companies will not let you send out direct mail pieces because the piece might be received by a person who is already a customer of another rep within the company. Some MLM companies consider this to be 'poaching' on another rep's business and it is not allowed.

An additional problem related to direct mail is the Do Not Mail List. People can sign up through the Direct Marketing Association to request that companies not send them marketing pieces. While this list is not legally enforced like the government's Do Not Call Registry (see next page), you would still be well advised not to mail to people on the list. Why? What do you think the chances are that someone will be interested in what you offer through a direct mail piece when they have taken the trouble to get their name on a Do Not Mail list? You are just wasting your precious advertising dollars. If you are going to do direct mail to a general list of consumers, have the company from which you buy the list run it against the Do Not Mail list to eliminate names and addresses that are on the Do Not Mail list.

- Insert mailers can be inexpensive; however, they are broadly targeted primarily by geography, and your ad can easily get lost among the two dozen or more ads inside the envelope.

- Do people want to be marketed to by phone? Approximately 100 million households have entered at least one telephone number into the U.S. governments Do Not Call Registry. With a projection of 112 million households for the U.S. in 2010, that means that almost 90% of households have indicated they don't want to receive telemarketing calls. As a business (small or otherwise), you cannot legally call a person at their place of residence if they have placed their name and number on the Do Not Call Registry. That means that for most cold calling, you will have to contact people at their place of work. The fact that people don't want you to call them at home to sell them something is also a good indicator of whether they are likely to want you to call them at work for the same purpose --- NOT!

- Email addresses are hard to get, unreliable, change frequently, and most emails end-up in the recipient's spam file and thus are never seen.

So, what's left? Renting a blimp is probably not a viable option, nor is getting your business name on a sports stadium.

You might consider ads on bus stop benches. Or you might consider getting your 'car wrapped' as a moving advertisement -- at a cost of $3,000-$10,000.

You can give away pens and calendars and coffee mugs. Of course, you still have the problem of getting in front of a person first before you can give them your freebie.

This brings us to the one way that most business leads for MLM businesses are generated, second only to cold calling people on the phone at their place of business --- Networking.

Networking is the term that is used (overused and misunderstood, actually) for meeting people in various business settings for the purpose of letting them know your business exists, and trying to start a 'relationship' where they might eventually buy your product, and you, theirs.

There are many types of networking groups. There are groups called 'leads/referral groups' where you pay to belong. Your membership in the group gives you an exclusive 'monopoly' on that particular kind of business within the group (i.e. only one real estate agent, only one chiropractor and only one insurance agent.) Groups such as LeTip and BNI are groups that have this format.

Unfortunately, these groups are often made up of only 20-30 different businesses, many of which are small, one-person companies. And, many will already have MLM businesses within them. It is not unusual to find a cosmetics MLM rep, a financial services MLM rep, a vitamin supplements or health juice rep, and perhaps a jewelry rep in the group.

The point is, the market within one of these groups is limited and that market has probably been approached by a number of other MLM reps. Unless you are selling a unique product or service, the market within the group will be limited.

The good news is that there is a lot of turnover within these groups. It is not unusual for a group to lose/replace 50-70% of its members within a year. That is good because it brings in fresh prospects for your product or service.

Nevertheless, this heavy turnover is also an indicator that these groups don't generate much business for their members. Think about it. If you were in one of these groups and you were getting a lot of business, wouldn't you stay in? But, if you weren't getting much business, wouldn't you move on to spend your advertising dollars in better and more effective ways?

The average annual membership fees for groups such as these are $300-$750 a year. In addition, with many of these groups, you <u>must</u> attend weekly luncheon or breakfast meetings as a requirement for keeping your membership. Add in the cost of 52 lunches or breakfasts (in the $10-$25 range depending on where the group holds its meetings and the part of the country in which you live), and you might find you will have annual expenses of $1,000 - $2,000 as your investment for being in the group.

In addition, most meetings in these groups last at least one and a half hours. Add in a half hour of commute time to get to the meeting, and a half hour to get back home/work after the meeting, and you will have invested over 130 hours a year in this networking option. That adds up to over three full business weeks (40 hour weeks) that you have used in advertising and marketing your business with this method.

That is not necessarily bad if you are generating enough business to justify the cost and time. But, you must ask yourself if there is a better way or place to invest that much time and money that might generate more business.

Other groups that provide networking opportunities would include Chambers of Commerce, Business Organizations and Associations, civic groups such as Rotary and Knights of Columbus, country clubs, and athletic clubs and teams. When you join one of these groups, keep in mind what the primary purpose of the group is. If it is heavily related to business development, networking and mutual referrals, it will be okay to proactively market your product or service.

Nevertheless, if the purpose of the group, association or organization is more civic, charity, or special purpose-oriented, you will have to take a more subtle approach to your sales activities.

I will address some more aspects of effective networking in Chapter 25.

Now, some of you are probably thinking: "*But what about marketing through a website?*"

It is true that many (if not most) MLM companies are going to provide you with some kind of 'personal website' from which to run your business. Since the Internet, Email, and websites are so visible today, I will talk about these in Chapter 25.

Chapter 11
Do you have to order, stock and deliver inventory?

If you are considering joining an MLM that sells a product(s), you will want to know who is responsible for processing the orders, keeping inventory in stock, and shipping or delivering the product to the end consumer.

The first question to answer is: "*Do I have to keep an inventory of product on hand from which to make shipments as the orders come in?*"

If you are selling women's jewelry, you might have to keep 'demo' stock available to show the pieces at parties. Each year, the inventory can change and you will have to buy new inventory to show. If this is the case, what do you do with the old inventory?

Do you sell it at a year-end closing sale? If yes, where can you hold a sale? Remember, you probably don't have an office or a store to which customers come. Thus, you will have to devise a way to get rid of out-dated stock or eat the costs.

Depending on the product, you might also have issues about keeping the product 'fresh'. Will that juice supplement be okay when it freezes while sitting on a customer's doorstep in Minnesota in February? Will that product be okay while being delivered in the 110 degree heat of Arizona in July? Can the packaging melt or freeze? How long is the expiration date on the product, and what happens if you don't sell it in time? Will the MLM Company take it back and reimburse you for your costs?

Other questions to consider are (1) whether you have to keep inventory on hand to fill orders; (2) whether you place each order for the customer; (3) is the order shipped to you for you to deliver; or (4), whether the product is shipped directly to the customer? The more you have to handle, store or ship/deliver the product to your customer, the more time it takes and the bigger the hassle it becomes.

If you have a choice, you might want to consider selling a product where either you or the customer places the order, and then the product is shipped directly to the customer. Processing, handling and shipping do not make you money. Actively selling to customers and prospects (or recruiting new team members) makes you money. The less time you have to spend with the logistics of the order, the more time you have to dedicate to selling. Keep this in mind when you select the product/service you are going to sell.

Chapter 12
Who provides customer service, especially when something goes wrong?

Regardless of the product or service, there are always things that might go wrong in delivering the final product or service to the end consumer. A question that you should consider is:

"Who handles the problems when they happen -- you or the MLM's Customer Service Department?"

What happens when the product or service doesn't deliver what was advertised? Does the customer call you, or do they call an actual Customer Service Department that is provided by the MLM Company? Depending on the product or service you are looking to sell, this can either be of little concern, or a gigantic headache.

Let's look at a couple of examples of MLM companies to see the difference in how a customer problem might be handled. First, let's look at a product like jewelry or a health supplement. If there is a problem with a necklace or a batch of vitamins, time is not a critical factor in solving the problem.

If the customer contacts you with the problem, you can either order new product or have 'corporate' send out replacement product. If that takes a day or two to happen, there is usually no great urgency or time demand by the customer in getting the problem fixed.

What if, however, you have decided to sell a product/service related to travel? If a customer arrives at his/her destination to find that the hotel room they reserved is not available, you/they have an immediate problem that needs to be fixed. In this situation, does the customer call you -- the rep -- at 1:00 a.m. in the morning to have you solve the problem? Or does the customer call a Customer Service Department that is trained and staffed 24/7/365 by 'headquarters' to deal with such issues?

Remember, in general, time you spend doing customer service is time when you are not able to be out actively selling. Nor is being awakened at all hours of the day or night going to do much for your overall productivity.

The point is, picking a product/service to sell that either (1) doesn't need much servicing or (2) where the MLM company handles the customer servicing, will probably put you on a better path to making the money you need to make from your MLM business.

Before you join an MLM, spend some time to determine who services the customer, you or the company? Then, decide whether having to be a Customer Service person who constantly handles problems and complaints is part of what you want in your MLM business.

Chapter 13
Who handles the accounting and paperwork?

Whether you are selling a product or a service, there will always be paperwork associated with setting up a new customer account and handling the accounting (ordering, billing, collecting) of the sales. Of course, in today's electronic environment, the old concept of paperwork has largely been replaced by on-line, electronic entry of the data.

Regardless of whether the setup and maintenance of accounts is handled electronically or by the old-fashioned paper method, someone has to do it. For the MLM companies you are considering joining, how is the setting up of accounts done and by whom?

In most companies, you will be the person who opens up the new account for your customer. Generally, this will be done through an on-line system (do you already have a computer on which you can do this, or will you have to purchase one?) If not on-line, then you will probably have to fax or mail-in the registration forms to get your new customer setup with an account.

If you are the person who has to open and setup the account, make sure you are going to get hands-on training from someone who has gone through the process many times before. While electronic systems are convenient, each has its own personality, glitches, nuances, and excuses -- *"we're working on that and it should be back on-line tomorrow."*

Unfortunately, you will have little choice (meaning -- none) or control over the systems that you will have to use that are provided by the company. If the computer systems are hard to understand and learn, always changing, constantly down with problems and bugs, it will be hard to run not only your own business, but it will be hard for the people you recruit to run theirs.

Look for systems that seem to be easy to understand and to operate, and which seem to be working most of the time that they are demonstrated to you. Ask some of the not-too-senior reps in the company about their personal experiences with the software systems provided by the company.

Don't ask too high up in the hierarchy because the higher you go, the more it is in their best interest to convince you that everything is 'hunky-dory', whether it really is or not. People down at the lowest levels, the newest recruits, are where you will get the most honest input about the computer systems the company provides.

There is another major issue about the accounting systems that you should consider: Who handles the ordering, billing, payments, and calculation and payment of commissions?

Let's deal with the orders first. Who orders the original product/service and who orders additional product in future purchases? In some MLM Companies (such as makeup for women), the sales rep talks with the customer, takes the order, places the order with headquarters, and then collects payment from the customer. In this situation, the rep is often purchasing 'product' from the MLM Company at a discount, marking the price up, and keeps the profit which is the difference between the price paid to the Company, and the price paid by the customer.

The point is, in this situation, the sales rep is heavily involved in the paperwork associated with making the sale and accounting for the receipts and commissions.

In some ways, this is good. If you are responsible for all the bookkeeping, you are in a position to make sure you get your rightful share of the proceeds. On the downside, doing all the paperwork takes time that is time you cannot be out selling even more.

For many MLM Companies, the orders are either (1) setup on a consistent, automated, "*keep-sending-it-until-I-tell-you-to-stop*" monthly schedule, or (2) the customer places the order directly. In either case, the rep is not directly involved in handling the orders, the billing, or the payments. In these cases, the rep receives a monthly accounting from the MLM Company, along with the commissions based on the orders placed and collected.

This certainly takes a lot of the hassle of handling the paperwork off the shoulders of the rep, and that is good. Unfortunately, the rep is trusting that the company will do the accounting accurately, ethically, and will calculate/pay the commissions that the rep rightfully deserves.

Many (if not most) of the commission plans for MLM companies are so complicated that even Einstein couldn't have determined if he got paid the right amount. (I will address the problems of Compensation Plans in more detail in Chapter 16).

The point is, make sure you are comfortable with the way your customers' orders are handled and the way your commissions are calculated and paid. If the particular MLM company you are thinking of joining has a confusing Comp Plan and total control of the billings, make sure you have some way to verify that you are being fairly paid for the sales you work so hard to generate.

Chapter 14
How much do you
<u>need</u> to make?

It is interesting how few people actually stop to think about how much they <u>need</u> to make from an MLM business. In truth, the answer to this question has more impact on whether you should get involved in an MLM (or any kind of business that you would own and operate) than any other question. So, now is the time for you to decide how much you <u>NEED</u> to make from an MLM business.

(<u>DISCLAIMER: The following methodology will calculate only rough estimates and are not to be used for tax or any other legal purposes. If you need more help in calculating your numbers, contact a qualified tax accountant or CPA. The author and publisher assume no responsibility for any legal or tax consequences you might incur due to actions you might take based on these calculations).</u>

Table 1

Monthly Expenses	Example Expenses	Your Expenses
Rent/Mortgage	$735.00	
Food		
At Home	$375.00	
Dining Out	$195.00	
Utilities		
Home Gas/Oil (Avg.)	$100.00	
Electricity (Avg.)	$65.00	
Telephones	$90.00	
Insurance		
Home/Renter	$75.00	
Car	$65.00	
Health	$115.00	
Life	$50.00	
Vehicle Gas	$100.00	
Internet/Cable/TV	$65.00	
Taxes/Registrations		
Home/Property	$66.00	
Car (Avg.)	$15.00	
Other	$5.00	
Clothing (Avg.)	$90.00	
Entertainment	$75.00	
Educational Expenses	0	
Charity Donations	$30.00	
Savings	$50.00	
Retirement Fund/IRA/KEOGH	$100.00	
All other miscellaneous	$100.00	
Total Monthly Expenses	$2,561.00	

There are many ways to decide how much you need to make. You can add up the monthly expenses for your household and that will be a good first target. But, there are other factors to consider. As a first step, fill out Table #1 as best you can.

(Please note that the expenses for your **household** are not to be confused with the expenses for the **business** that were discussed in Chapter 9).

In this example, we have a household that has estimated monthly expenses of $2,561. This equates to annual expenses of $30,732 ($2,561 * 12 months = $30,732).

Once you have done your best to estimate your monthly expenses, you will need to determine your approximate income tax rate before you can calculate how much you must make in gross earnings to be able to net the amount of your monthly expenses.

The simplest way to calculate an estimated tax rate is to take the total amount of taxes you paid on your latest income tax returns (combined total of Federal and State income taxes paid including Social Security) and divide that by the total amount of income (after deducting allowable business expenses) you reported on your income tax return.

If our example household paid a combined total of $7,340 of state and federal taxes, and had $38,795 of total gross income (after expenses), the estimated tax rate for purposes of our calculations would be 18.9% ($7,340 / $38,795 = 18.9%).

Please note that our example household had Net Income <u>after</u> taxes of approximately $31,455 ($38,795 - $7,340 = $31,455). The good news is that for this example household, the net income after taxes ($31,455) was slightly more than the estimated annual household expenses ($30,732). Once you have calculated your expenses and your tax rate, you are then ready to determine how much you <u>NEED</u> to make from an MLM business.

(Once you get to this point in your calculations, this might be a good time to sit down with your tax professional to make sure your estimates are accurate enough for your planning purposes.)

Let's assume that you are planning to do an MLM business on a part-time basis while continuing to work at your day job (or your night job if that is when you work at your regular job). Let's also assume that you have estimated monthly household expenses of $2,000 and current net income from your existing job of $1,750 per month. To calculate how much you need to make from your MLM job to yield the additional $250 needed, fill out Table 2 using the example as a guide.

In our example, to calculate the "*Gross Income Required to Net Additional Income Needed*", we divide the "*Additional Net Income Needed*" -- $250, by the "*Net Income Percentage*" -- 81.10%. This calculation yields $308.26.

What this means is, based on your income tax rate of 18.9%, you will have to earn approximately $308.26 per month of additional gross income to yield additional net income of $250 after taxes.

But, what if you don't have a current job and income? You can still do these calculations using the income tax rate from your last job. Remember, these are only rough estimates to give you an idea of approximately how much you need to make from an MLM job. **Again, if you need help with your numbers, consider spending $50-$100**

for an hour of a tax accountant's time. It will be money well spent.

Table 2

	Example	**Yours**
Estimate Monthly Expenses	$2,000	
Current Monthly Net Income	$1,750	
Additional Net Income Needed	$250	
Gross Income Percentage	100.00%	
Income Tax Rate	18.90%	
Net Income Percentage	81.10%	
Gross Income Required to Net Additional Income Needed	$308.26	

Table 3 shows an example based on <u>not having any income</u> from an existing job. We will use the tax rate calculated from Table 1 based on this person's last job.

The "*Gross Income Required to Net Additional Income Needed*" of $2,000 after taxes is approximately $2,466.09 assuming an 18.90% tax rate ($2,000 / 18.9% = $2,466.09).

Thus, if you need to pay $2,000 of monthly <u>household</u> expenses from an MLM business, you will have to generate commissions/income, after expenses, of approximately $2,500.

Table 3

Example **Yours**

	Example	Yours
Estimate Monthly Expenses	$2,000	
Current Monthly Net Income	$0	
Additional Net Income Needed	$2,000	
Gross Income Percentage	100.00%	
Income Tax Rate	18.90%	
Net Income Percentage	81.10%	
Gross Income Required to Net Additional Income Needed	$2,466.09	

Please note that this is **~$2,500 of commissions, NOT SALES**! If you are selling a product/service that pays a 25% percent commission, you would have to generate total sales of $10,000 per month to generate commissions of $2,500. ($2,500 / 25% = $10,000).

Let me reiterate that the $2,500 is what you need to make AFTER BUSINESS EXPENSES! If your deductible expenses for the business are $1,000 per month and you have a 25% commission rate, you will need to have total sales of ~$11,000 per month to net $2,500 per month after taxes and expenses.

At this point, some of you may feel that this is all pretty confusing. Please understand that it is not my intent to confuse you. Quite to the contrary. My intent is to help you understand your basic financial needs so that you can determine if getting into an MLM is a good solution.

More importantly, **until you have all the numbers relative to your situation, and until you understand all the numbers in the examples above, you probably shouldn't get into an MLM business** (or any other kind of business for that matter.)

For many of you, these numbers will be common-sense stuff that you already understand. For those of you who don't understand these numbers and calculations, that's okay. Just don't rush into an MLM (or any other kind of business) until you do understand them. You will save yourself a lot of grief and financial problems if you will understand these examples and calculate your own needs before investing your time, money, and energy in an MLM business.

Chapter 15
How much will an 'average' rep make in an MLM Company?

Now that you have calculated the amount of commissions, income, and/or bonuses you need to earn to pay your monthly household expenses, the next logical question is, what is the likelihood that you might make that amount by getting into an MLM business?

Obviously, if you only need to make an extra $200 of net income, the chances are pretty good. Nevertheless, if you need to generate a full salary like $48,000, (12 months * $4,000 = $48,000/Yr.), the odds just got significantly lower that you might make that kind of money in an MLM.

What most people who are considering getting into an MLM business would probably like to know is: "*What is likely to be the <u>Real Income</u> for an 'Average' Rep in an MLM business?*"

But, of course, therein lies some of the problem. Most people believe they will be 'above average' at things they undertake when they compare themselves to everyone else. Garrison Keillor of *"Prairie Home Companion"* fame made this idea humorous when he said that "*Lake Wobegon is a place where all the children are above average.*"

Unfortunately, everyone cannot be 'above average'. In fact, it is a mistaken belief that even half of the people will be 'above average'.

Let's look at Table 4 which shows this problem with 'averages'.

As Table 4 shows, the <u>average</u> commission for all 10 reps is $2000 ($20,000 / 10 = $2,000). Yet, in truth, only one rep makes an 'above average' commission -- Larry. The other nine make less than the average.

You might think that the numbers shown in this table are unrealistic. Based on the numbers shown, Larry receives 55% of all the commissions being paid ($11,000 / $20,000 = 55%). In this example, Larry represents the Top 10% of commissions earners (1 rep / 10 reps = 10%) but he receives 55% of total commissions.

Unfortunately, in many MLM companies, the Top **1%** of reps earn about 50% of all commissions (No, that is not a typo. The Top **ONE** percent of reps earn 50% of total commissions.) In some MLM companies, the Top 1% earn over 70% of all commissions!

Why is this so important to note? There are a number of reasons why you should take special note of this issue before you decide to buy into an MLM business.

First, the MLM companies make a special effort to advertise the earnings of the <u>top reps</u> as a way to get you to believe (and hope) that you, too, might make HUGE money in an MLM business. Of course, as many of MLM Companies own numbers verify, only the Top 1% are making BIG money.

Table 4

Name	Commissions	% of Total Commissions
Annie	$1000	5%
Bill	$1000	5%
Clyde	$1000	5%
Don	$1000	5%
Erin	$1000	5%
Faith	$1000	5%
George	$1000	5%
Harry	$1000	5%
Jack	$1000	5%
Larry	$11,000	55%
Total	$20,000	100%
Average	$2,000	

(Note: During the usual one-hour sales/recruiting presentation by an MLM company, you will hear 59 minutes related to the big money earners, and two, 30-second disclaimers that say something to the effect that: "*These numbers do not represent typical results. Your actual earnings will vary depending on the amount of effort you put into your business.*")

Don't be dazzled and fooled by all the hype about the big earners. You are not likely to be one of them. It is similar to how lotteries are advertised. You always here about the big winners but you never see or hear about the millions of losers.

The second reason you should take note is that the MLM companies will also suggest that <u>anyone</u> can make it into the Top 1%. You will be given examples of hair-dressers, waiters, single Mom's, retired grandmothers and other seemingly 'average' people who are supposedly making big money. While there might be a few (exceedingly few -- as in one in 10,000) people who are the exception, the truth is that the 'average' person has little hope of making even a decent income from an MLM business, let alone making it into the Top 1%.

Yet, it is the mere hope that you might be that one person in 10,000 that allows these companies to churn through a seemingly never-ending stream of people, only to have 9,999 of them end up feeling like failures because they couldn't make enough to break even after expenses.

That is what most MLM companies sell -- HOPE. Could you be that one person in 10,000 who makes it big? Yes, but those one in 10,000 people have specific skills and characteristics, some of which you might not be able to acquire no matter how smart or hard-working you might be. If you do not possess those characteristics, your odds of being that one person in 10,000 who makes it big are nil.

<u>If you think these statements are inaccurate, all you have to do is look at the numbers that many of the MLM companies provide in their 'Disclosure Statements'</u>.

(By the way, many MLM Companies provide their Disclosure Statements online. Others hand them out at the 'recruiting events'. Try to get a copy of the disclosure statement for the MLM you are considering buying into. If they won't give you one or don't have one, **beware**! If they won't share their numbers, there is probably a reason they don't want you to see them.)

Table 5 is an example of what one of these 'disclosure statements' might show:

What do all these numbers really mean? Let's walk through some calculations to get a better understanding of how likely it is for the 'average independent representative' of this MLM Company to make some big money.

Table 5

Success Levels	High Annual Commiss.	Low Annual Commiss.	Average Annual Commiss.	% Who Reach Level
Qualified Rep	$4,000	$10	$116.00	17.2%
Sr. Rep.	$16,000	$100	$2,400	2.0%
Director/Mgr.	$58,000	$2,200	$21,000	0.32%
Reg. Director	$210,000	$95,000	$140,000	0.017%
Natl. Director	$310,000	$190,000	$260,000	0.007%
Intl. Director	$1,090,000	$310,000	$525,000	0.004%

Suppose that you are about to join this company when it has been in business for a couple of years and currently has 100,000 active reps. The first thing you need to understand is that this is actually the number of **'STILL ACTIVE'** reps.

It is possible (and highly likely) that this company has actually signed up anywhere from 150,000-200,000 reps or more during the time it has been in business. Of course, the company is unlikely to tell you how many reps have signed in total. Why? Because that just makes the numbers look much different --- and much worse.

According to this disclosure statement you would be led to believe that 17.2% of the reps of the company reach the *"Qualified Rep"* level. This is incorrect. If we multiply 17.2% times the 100,000 <u>active</u> reps, 17,200 reps are <u>currently</u> at the Qualified Rep Level.

In truth, we would have to take the 17,200 people who are <u>still active</u> who reached the QR level and divide them by the total number of reps who <u>EVER</u> joined the company. Let's assume that number was 200,000. Therefore, the truth is, only 8.6% of all reps ever reach the QR level. (17,200 / 200,000 = 8.6%)

Let's make sure you understand what that means. It means that less than one person out of 10 who joins the company will reach even the first level of commissions where **the average ANNUAL commission check is --- $116.00**!

I want to repeat this one more time because this is the single most important piece of information you need to consider before you invest your time and energy in an MLM company. For the example above:

Less than one person out of 10 who joins this MLM company will earn an annual income of $116 --- PER YEAR!

The rest receive less --- or nothing!

Let's put this into further perspective. If you add up the percentages in the right hand column of Table 5 you get a total of 19.548%. But, again, those percentages are calculated based on 100,000 active reps. If we take the 19,548 (19.548% * 100,000) active reps who make some kind of commission and divide that by the 200,000 people who <u>ever</u> joined the company, <u>only 9.8% earn any commission, less than one out of 10</u>, and that's <u>BEFORE EXPENSES</u>!

Thus, of the people who sign-on to become an independent rep for this company, 90.2% will earn basically nothing, and that is before taking into account the expenses associated with the business! Wow! That's quite a difference between what you will hear and see advertised, and the reality of how many people will actually get wealthy in the business.

But, it gets even worse. Only 0.348% (that's one-third of one percent) of the active reps make Director or higher. That means that only 348 people, out of the original 200,000 got to the Director level. Directors make, on average, $252,000 a year. Now, that's darn good money. No question about it.

The question is, how likely are <u>you</u> to get to be one of them? Not very likely. Furthermore, what the table doesn't show you is how long Directors have been with the company.

If you ask around, you are likely to find that most of the people who are at Director level or higher signed up (1) during the first six months the company was in business, or (2) before the company even launched its product/service to the general public --- and <u>there is no way at this point for you to become one of them</u>. Remember, in this example, you were joining a couple of years into the deal.

Ask the independent rep or team leader who is trying to recruit you for his/her team to find out how many of the people who have signed up in the last year have reached Director level out of how many who signed up in total --- but don't expect to get an answer. They probably don't know, and can't/won't find out.

Why? Because it is likely that out of the 348 Directors, fewer than a dozen of them have been with the company for less than a year. And, if you were to be able to get the real data, you would likely find that those people who reached Director level in less that a year are friends or family members of a Director above them who is helping them out.

Remember these numbers when you hear all those big numbers that are touted, spouted and shouted at the 'recruitment' presentations. The numbers that are shown in the event won't look nearly so great when you get to see all the numbers. Unfortunately, we're still not done with the bad news.

Continuing with our example, there are only 17 Regional Directors, 7 National Directors, and 4 International Directors. And, you can bet your bottom dollar that they all joined the company in the very beginning. In fact, not only did they join early, they were most likely hand-picked and recruited by the founders/developers/owners of the business before the company was even launched.

One of the things that you will hear stated at recruitment events is "*the tremendous experience of the execu-*

tive/management team." They will have *"75-150-200"* years of combined experience in MLM companies.

Of course they will. Why? Because they were all in MLM companies before this one and this 'good old boy/girl club' often moves from one company to the next as they develop one company, rake in the easy earnings, cash-out, and then move on to the next one where their success is virtually guaranteed because they always get in at the very beginning.

Of course, <u>you</u> are unlikely to ever have the chance to get in at the <u>real</u> beginning because you aren't part of the club. In truth, even if you join a company that has a 'Launch Date' a few months out, most of the people at the top have already been hand-picked; and many are already putting their teams in place. Basically speaking, if you aren't already in the club, you're unlikely to ever get in.

If the real money (remember, the Top 1% will take in 50%-70% of all the commissions) is made by a hand-picked team that gets in before day one, what does that leave for those who get in later? Not much. Certainly not the <u>big</u> bucks.

What are your real chances of getting past the Director Level? Your chances are <u>not</u> 28 out of 200,000 (17+7+4 = 28). No. Those 28 have been in from the 'pre-early' days and those 'pre-early' days are gone. The only thing left to be fought over now are the scraps. Your chances of getting past the Director Level are probably the same as your chances of winning a Million Dollar Lottery --- next to zero.

Nevertheless, as we all know, someone will win the lottery. Unfortunately, we only hear about the tiny number of winners. We never hear about the millions of losers.

That is why I have written this book. I want you to determine whether you have what it takes to be the exception in the world of MLM businesses. If you find that you are that exceptional person, then go for it and best of luck.

But, please understand that, even if you do possess the required characteristics, the amount of time, effort, commitment, persistence, and dedication that is required to become a multi-millionaire in MLM is no different from any other kind of business. What you get out of it is determined by the amount of effort you put into it.

If you find that you do not have the characteristics that I listed in Chapter 3, I would suggest that you consider saving your money and your feelings, and consider getting a regular job where you are not responsible for being the sole creator of sales as you will be in an MLM business.

Chapter 16
Can you understand the compensation plan?

If you think that some of the topics I have discussed thus far are confusing and complicated, "*You ain't seen nothin' yet!*" Many of the 'Compensation Plans' for MLM companies represent the most confusing way to get paid that has probably ever been conceived. Unfortunately, a lot of this confusion is by intent and by design. <u>Many MLM companies do not want you to be able to understand their comp plan</u>.

You should also read the 'fine print' in a document that will generally be referred to as the "*Policies and Procedures Manual*", or something similar in wording. The key words to watch for in these "Policies and Comp Plans" are:

"*The Company has the total and unilateral right to change any and all aspects of this Policies and Procedures Manual, and the Compensation Plan, at any time, without recourse by the Independent Representatives.*"

This means that the company can change any aspect of its agreement with you, at any time, for no reason at all other than it wants to. You will have no say in the matter, and you will have no legal basis to challenge the Company's decisions and actions.

Even if you understand and agree to all the policies, procedures, and the Compensation Plan when you first join the company, be aware that the company might be able to change any/all aspects, at will, whenever it chooses to do so.

In truth (and unfortunately this has happened to more than a few independent sales reps), you might spend three-five years building a huge team and making thousands of dollars a month, and have it all taken away tomorrow with a single swipe of the Company's 'magic legal pen'.

Will it happen? Maybe. Can it happen? Yes. So, just beware of all the hype about "*setting yourself up to receive a great residual income in the future.*" If the company is still around, maybe you will receive your hard-earned rewards. But, there are absolutely no promises that the company will adhere to the current policies or pay schedule in the future.

(PLEASE NOTE: Many MLM companies will try to get you to "*Sign-up today so you don't miss out on this unbelievable opportunity!*" If you read the 'contract' that you are about to sign, even if it is online, you would see a place where it says something like:

"*By signing this document, you agree that you have been given and have read and understood the Policies and Procedures Manual, the Comp Plan, the Disclosure Statement, and all related documents."*

If you sign that contract, you are admitting that you have been given all the relevant information and have read and understood it --- even if you haven't! In a court of law, your signature on that paper is the only relevant evidence, and an admission by you that you read the contract and related materials. <u>The fact that you didn't ask for them or didn't read them is your problem!</u> So:

<u>Ask for all the legal documents</u>
<u>from the company, read them,</u>
<u>and understand them,</u>
<u>BEFORE YOU SIGN!</u>

It's as simple as that.

Ignore the hype about "*missing out on the opportunity if you don't sign today.*" The recruiter will be saying the same exact thing to the people he/she tries to recruit tomorrow, next week and next year.

Now, having said that, if you choose to get into an MLM company, you need to understand the Comp Plan or you will have no idea whether you can earn the money you need to make.

<u>Different Types of Comp Plans</u>

How many different kinds of Comp Plans are there? About the same number as the number of MLM companies. Each company has its own twists and nuances to its Comp Plan.

Nevertheless, there are a few basic types of Comp Plans that you should know about and understand before you select the MLM Company you will join. Some of the most common plans include:

1. Matrix Plans
2. Stairstep Breakaway Plans
3. Unilevel Plans
4. Binary Plans
5. Australian Two-Up Plans

I am not going to go into a lot of detail to explain the aspects of the various plans. There are too many variations to cover. Needless to say, you need to be able to understand the plan for the company you are considering joining.

Since these plans are always changing and new ones are being added, I suggest you go on the Internet and use Google to search on *"MLM Compensation Plans."* You will find a number of reports and articles about the latest, greatest (and worst) forms of compensation plans currently in use.

You should also look up the Comp Plan for the specific MLM companies you are considering joining, if you haven't yet been given them. Or ask the person who is trying to recruit you to give you a copy of the Comp Plan and the "Policies and Procedures Manual."

Regardless of where you search for more detailed answers, there are some basics about these plans that you should make sure you understand.

MLM -- Is Multi-Level Marketing Right for You?

In most plans, you sign up people in the next level below you (that's why it's called Multi-Level Marketing and not direct sales). Those people then sign up people in the next level below them, and so on. It looks similar to an organizational chart in a company:

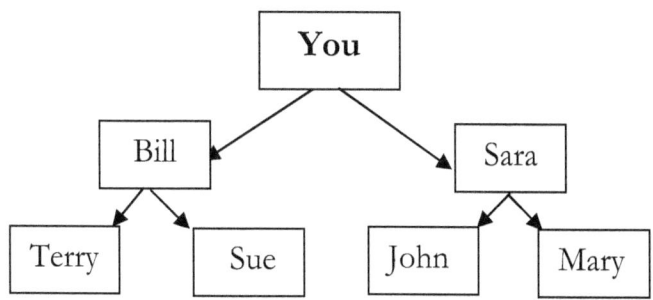

In this simple diagram, you are at the top and there are two levels of people under you. There is only one level under Bill, and no levels under Terry.

This simple diagram also shows what is known as a Binary Setup. Under each person, there are only two lines. Every new person has to be added at the bottom of one of the levels. Thus, if Jenny signed on next, she would have to appear under Terry, Sue, John or Mary.

One of the advantages of a binary plan that will be stated by the MLM's that offer this kind of plan is that every new person has to go under someone on the existing line. Thus, in the example above, if Jenny decides to join, she has to go under either Terry, Sue, John or Mary, and everyone above Jenny on that direct line might get some credit for her having joined. Jenny cannot be placed in between Sarah and John or between Bill and You.

In some ways that is good for you. If you are Sue or Terry and someone above you (like Bill) recruits a new person, that new person will have to go somewhere at the bottom of either your team, or at the bottom of another rep's team, and you might get some financial benefits from Jenny having been put below you.

The MLM recruiters will try to impress you by telling you how you can join today, and you might not have to do <u>any</u> work because the people above you will continue to add people under you without your having to do anything.

While that sounds good on paper, in reality, it just doesn't work that way. The huge percentage of new recruits is added from the 'warm leads list' of the last group of recruits who joined. (See Chapter 21 for more info about the 'Warm Leads List'.) Seldom (more likely, never) will the people above you add people onto your team. It is the new recruits and their 'warm lists' of prospects on the lowest level of the pyramid who will be adding the vast majority of new recruits.

People in your 'upline' will state that they personally signed up only 5 or 10 or maybe 25 people. Yet, they will simultaneously talk about putting people 'under you' as they sign up new ones. The truth is, your upline will seldom if ever be signing up any new recruits and putting them under you!

And, even if they do occasionally sign up a new recruit themselves, they can put that new recruit below <u>any</u> person in their downline, of which you may be one of a 100 or 1,000 from which they can pick.

The point is, <u>don't plan on having your team built for you by the people above you. It just won't happen.</u>

Now, let's continue with some additional information about comp plans in general.

In some plans, there are multiple 'legs' under each person. This might look like the following:

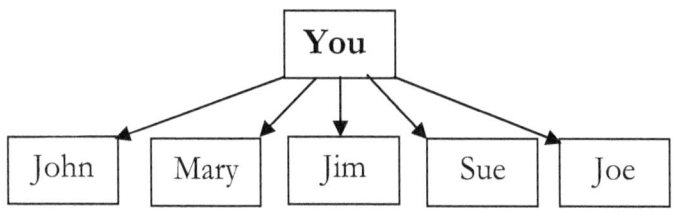

In this example, there are five legs under you. Currently, there are no legs under any of the people below you.

The number of legs varies based on the company and the compensation plan. The maximum is usually around seven, but two legs (binary) and three legs are common.

The commissions that you might earn are tied directly to the levels under you. In some plans, you will receive commissions from all the sales made below you for the first three, five, or perhaps seven levels. For some plans you might receive 10% of sales from the first level, 5% from the second level, and 2% for all levels down to seven.

In another plan the percentages might be reversed. In that kind of plan you might receive 2% of sales from the first level, 5% from the second through sixth levels, and 10% for all levels from seven on down.

In some plans, especially Binary Plans, you might receive commissions for an infinite number of levels below you. But, in these types of plans, you often receive commissions only as long as a minimum number of sales or new recruits are added each month. Thus, you only earn money if your team keeps growing.

In many plans, you have to 'keep your legs balanced' to receive the highest commissions (and, in some cases, in order to receive any commissions at all.)

For example, you might find yourself in a Plan with three legs under you and a total of 3,000 people on your team. Unfortunately, if the Comp Plan for this company states that you have to keep your three legs 'balanced' to receive commissions, you might have 50 on Leg 1, 50 on Leg 2 and 2,900 on Leg 3 (where you got lucky and signed on a super-salesperson) and, therefore, you might only receive commissions based on 150 recruits in total (only 50 each from Legs 1, 2, and 3 would be 'balanced'). The rest of the 2,850 recruits under Leg 3 are put into a 'holding area' with hopes that you will get more recruits in Legs 1 and 2 to balance them out.

Unfortunately, there is often a limited time period (perhaps six months or a year) attached to those 2,850 extra recruits. To get the commissions linked to those recruits, you have to get the legs balanced within a given time. In other words, you have to get an additional 2,850 on both Leg 1 and Leg 2 (5,700 additional recruits) or lose the extra recruits in Leg 3 and the commissions associated with them.

Are you getting a little confused? Well, don't feel like you're the only person who can't/doesn't understand these Comp Plans. As I mentioned in an earlier chapter, many (if not most) of the MLM Comp Plans are so confusing that even Einstein might have had trouble figuring them out.

As I also mentioned before, many Comp Plans are intentionally designed to be confusing and hard to figure out. In truth, many MLM's would prefer that you take them at their word that "*you can make a huge pile of money in their company.*" As we have already seen, this is generally not the case; and, the more confusing they make the Comp Plans, the better off they are -- at your expense.

The main question to answer is, can you easily and clearly understand how, and how much you will earn based on the particular Comp Plan that is being offered by the company you think you will join? If yes, then, no worries.

However, if you can't understand the Comp Plan, **beware**. If you can't understand the Comp Plan in less than five minutes, you probably should look for a different company with a simpler plan. In general, the companies with simple plans have lasted longer. Those companies are in for the long-haul, which is what you want if you intend to make your MLM business your career.

When all is said and done, here are some aspects you would like to find in the Comp Plan for the company you are thinking of joining:

1. The Comp Plan is simple and easy to understand.
2. You are given a bonus for every new customer.
3. You are given a bonus for every new 'recruit' you sign who plans to build his/her own team under you.

4. You receive a percentage of the initial product/service sales that you make from your own customers.
5. You receive a bonus for every new customer signed on by your team.
6. You receive a percentage of the initial product/service sales that your team members make from their customers.
7. You receive bigger commissions when you and your team reach higher levels of sales.
8. You receive 'residual' commissions or income from future sales once you have built and maintain your team at a certain level(s) of sales or revenue.

Be aware that you will seldom get all of these things in any MLM company's Comp Plan. But, that doesn't mean you shouldn't go for as much as you can. After all, unless you are getting into an MLM as a hobby or for social networking, your primary aim is to make money. Make sure you can make the money you want in return for the time and effort you will put in.

Chapter 17
The 'Momentum Phase' of an MLM Company

If you attend a few 'presentations' by MLM companies, sooner or later you will get to see the diagram that shows the four stages of a 'successful MLM business'. According to Charles King, PhD, Professor of Marketing at the University of Illinois, every successful MLM company goes through 4 growth phases (with estimated annual revenues listed in parentheses):

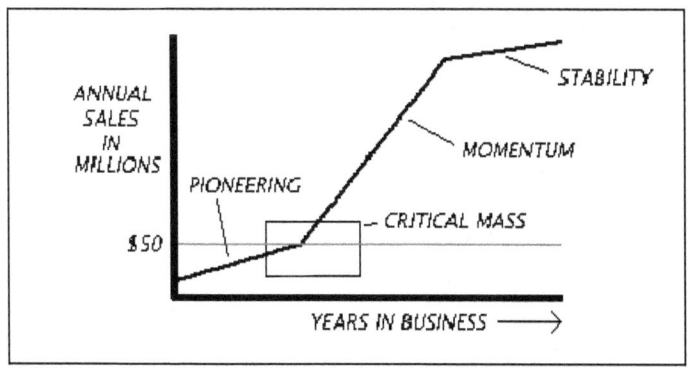

The four phases are:

1. Formulation (or Pioneering - $0 to $20 Million)
2. Concentration ($20 Million to $40 Million)
   --- Critical Mass (approximately $50 Million)
3. Momentum ($50 Million to $500 Million, maybe close to $1 Billion)
4. Stability (>$500 Million, sometimes at or above $1 Billion)

According to Dr. King, an MLM company goes through several major growth phases as it matures into a stable, long-term opportunity. The first growth stage is known as the "formulation stage." This is the start-up phase when companies are most vulnerable and over 90% go out of business within 12-24 months.

The second phase of growth is referred to as the "concentration phase." During concentration, the company is still getting its business lined up and working out the bugs. Similar to the formulation phase, the concentration phase is still considered a start-up phase and is a risky time to get involved. These two phases are often referred to as "pioneering" and most experts agree that the risk-to-reward ratio is high.

According to Dr. King, if a company reaches approximately $50 million in annual sales, the company experiences a phenomenon known as "critical mass." This figure should not be taken too literally and could occur slightly before or slightly after the first $50 million, bringing with it the beginning of the company's "momentum growth phase." During this phase, if the foundation was properly laid, a company can go from obscurity to becoming a household name within 3 to 5 years.

Please note that the growth of an MLM company into the Momentum phase has <u>lots of if's</u> attached to it. Most MLM companies never reach or sustain their growth into the momentum phase.

What does this have to do with your deciding whether to get into an MLM company or not? You will be amazed at how many companies just happen to be "*in or about to entering the Momentum stage where the explosive growth happens!*" It is amazing how often this timing will conveniently coincide with the time when <u>you</u> are being recruited into the business.

The point the MLM companies will emphasize about this chart is that "*you'd better get in before the big explosion happens. You don't want to look back a couple of years from now and have to tell yourself that you could have gotten in before the company went global*".

Is this information true? Yes, it seems to be. But, the critical word that must be noted is that these are the growth phases of '<u>successful</u>' MLM companies. Unfortunately, most MLM companies never get that far. Let me take a moment here to tell you about a concept called the "*Survivorship Bias*".

Suppose 100 MLM companies were started exactly ten years ago. As with any other type of business, 50-60% will not make it through the first year. Thus, at the end of year one, we had only 50 of the original 100 still in operation.

Only one in 10 is likely to survive to still be in existence after ten years. Thus, after year ten, only 10 out of the original 100 are likely to still be in business.

If we examine those 10 at the end of ten years, they might all look pretty successful and profitable. But, those 10 are <u>not representative</u> of all the MLM businesses that were started ten years ago. They are simply the 'survivors'. Thus, the apparent success that those 10 present are biased because they only represent the survivors. We do not see any of the statistics (lost investments and bankruptcies) of the other 90 businesses which are no longer around.

This concept of survivorship bias applies both to the business, and to the individual reps in the business. As was previously discussed, the MLM companies will talk about the 'Active' reps in the company. These are actually the 'still active survivors'. They will represent only a small percentage of the total reps who were ever involved with the company.

In addition, the fact that the 10 MLM companies survived for 10 years does not mean that any of them reached the 'Momentum' phase that would define them as being 'successful'.

What is the point of this discussion? When you go to a recruitment presentation, the odds are you will get to see the "Momentum Phase" chart as a way to convince you that this company (and you by becoming a part of it) is going to <u>explode</u> onto the market place and make everyone in it a fortune.

Sorry, but that just isn't true. And the companies' own numbers prove it.

So, don't be mislead by all the hype, glitz and shouting of the big numbers. Remember, the MLM companies always tout the survivors. They never speak about the

MLM -- Is Multi-Level Marketing Right for You?

99% of the reps who either didn't survive, or who didn't make enough to buy a cup of coffee after expenses.

Unless you possess the right characteristics and get in at the very beginning of the company, your chances of being one of the top 1% are still virtually nil.

Hawkeye Richardson

Chapter 18
Other important issues to consider

There are a number of other questions that you might want to ask before you decide to get into an MLM, or before you decide which MLM will work best for you. In no particular order, here are some other issues to consider.

1. If you have a regular day job (or a night job if you happen to work the night shift), will joining an MLM have any negative impact on that job?

2. If your boss(es) find out, will they care?

3. Will it have any negative impact on your 'image' at work, either personally or professionally, that might place your regular job in jeopardy?

4. Will you have to be careful <u>not</u> to advertise or market yourself at work, and not to approach your co-workers at work or outside of work?

5. Will working at an MLM job use up precious time and energy that you need to do your regular job well?

6. How are your close friends and family going to feel about your being in an MLM? Will they be supportive? Skeptical? Will they feel that you are abusing your relationship with them if you approach them to buy your product or service, or to join your team? How much is your friendship with them worth versus any possible negatives your involvement in an MLM might create?

7. Can you belong to more than one MLM? Some people sell non-competing products and services from multiple MLM's as a way to make enough money to meet their needs, especially when they discover that they can't make enough from working just one MLM. Nevertheless, some MLM companies do not want you to carry multiple MLM products (they feel it will distract you and lessen the amount of time you dedicate to theirs.) If you decide to join more than one MLM, make sure the ones you join allow it.

8. Can you 'will' your MLM business to your heirs? Hey, if you work hard and get into some serious money, your MLM business might be worth a lot of money. You would want your heirs to be able to inherit the business and continue to work it or receive any 'residual' income you may have earned.

9. Can you sell your MLM business in the open market? If you develop your MLM into a substantial business

and then decide you want to 'retire' or 'get out', make sure you have the right to sell it. Some MLM companies force you to sell your 'business' back to the company. If that is the case for the MLM you are considering joining, make sure you are comfortable (happy) with the deal they will offer if you have to sell it back to the company.

10. Are you comfortable with doing recruiting or sales parties in your home or apartment? Recognize that often, multiple reps will put on a cooperative event at one person's home as a way to reduce costs and generate more excitement (it is harder to get two people excited than it is to generate a buzz with 20 people in the room). Unfortunately, that means that you are going to have a lot of strangers in your home. Some thieves go to recruiting events to 'scope out' the house for later theft. In addition, your home owner's (or renter's) insurance policy seldom covers liability or theft associated with a business you are operating out of your home. If a person attends a sales/recruiting event and falls on the ice outside your home, or trips over the projector cord and breaks a leg, you are liable. A homeowner's policy also does not usually cover business inventory you might store in your home or garage. You might need/want to get a separate liability/theft insurance policy to cover your MLM business.

11. Will any product you have to keep in inventory or store in your home or car be damaged by excessive dust, heat or cold?

12. How many hours a week can you comfortably commit to your MLM business? Will this amount of time have a negative impact on the time you have for your regular work, time with spouse, friends and family, or other time commitments you already have? (church, athletics, school, organizations, charitable work).

13. How will you feel if you invest your heart and soul, and your time and energy (not to mention a considerable amount of money) into your MLM business, only to have it turn out to be a bust? Remember that extremely few people will make it big in an MLM, and few earn enough even to make a comfortable living. If you are doing this for fun or social reasons, okay. But, if you are doing this because you <u>need</u> the money, give serious consideration to all the things that have been discussed in this book.

Too many people get into an MLM with great hopes for becoming a millionaire in a matter of months. Only one in 10,000 have a chance of reaching that level of earnings. If you don't have the characteristics of a person who is likely to succeed at an MLM business, don't jump into an MLM only to feel like a huge failure if it doesn't work out.

PART 2:
What to Do After Joining an MLM

Chapter 19
How do you feel about making 'Cold Calls'?

At this point, you have identified a product or service that you are going to sell. You have identified the target market for this product. The next question to answer is:

"How are you going to make contact with the people in your Target Market group?"

MLM companies often use the term 'direct sales' to describe how their products and services get marketed. They will state that *"You -- the independent sales rep -- are our sales force. This product or service practically sells itself, and word-of-mouth is the most effective form of advertising that has ever been found."*

These statements are, at least from a legal standpoint, mostly true. Unfortunately, while they might be true, they do not clearly represent how MLM sales really work.

In an MLM business, you -- the independent sales rep -- will generally have to have direct, person-to-person, or at least voice-to-voice, contact with your potential customer. If you were an actual employee for a company (they hired you and paid you a salary), you would be called -- a salesperson. But, of course, the MLM companies know that most people hate selling or being considered a - SALESPERSON!

Many MLM Companies say that you will become an "Independent Consultant". Those are just fancy words they use to make you believe you won't be a salesperson. Don't believe it. Regardless of the name/title, a salesperson is exactly what you will be.

Of course, being a <u>salesperson</u> means you have to do things like --- make cold calls on the phone to setup appointments so that you can hawk your wares. Unfortunately, few people like to make cold calls (even most natural born sales-types hate making cold calls. In fact, it is generally believed that anyone who actually likes to make cold calls is probably an alien!)

Surely that is not what you have to do as the independent rep for an MLM company, is it? Sorry, but that is EXACTLY what you will have to do! As an MLM rep, you are unlikely to have a storefront or office to which customers/prospects will come to buy your products. Just like any other business, you will have to get your butt in gear and go out and rustle up prospects.

Now, that's not necessarily bad. We are all salespeople in various ways. We are always selling various things and ideas to our spouses, our children, our friends and family, our co-workers, and lots of other people. But, it is one thing to convince someone you know to buy something you have or to do something you want/need them to do. It is another thing entirely to convince strangers to do what you want, including, to buy the MLM product/service you are selling.

How are you going to setup appointments to sell your product/service to your prospects?

Here is where the MLM companies will try to fool you into believing that selling their product or service is as easy as falling off a log. But, ask yourself this question: What usually happens when someone falls off a log? Sometimes, they get hurt.

You are probably not going to get physically hurt selling most MLM products. Nevertheless, it is possible to be emotionally and psychologically 'injured', and your ego might take a real beating if you don't know what you are getting yourself into. So, let's take a moment to see how many MLM companies 'teach' their independent reps to set appointments.

Most MLM companies will start you off by having you put together a list of all the people you know to whom you could place a phone call (at work) to give your 30-second sales pitch. (This is often referred to as your 'warm leads list' which I will discuss in a moment.) The more people you know, the better. But, this list is not limited to close friends and family. Oh, no. You are instructed to list EVERYONE you know or have ever known.

Family; friends; co-workers; the mailman; your hairdresser or barber; the people who graduated with you from high school and college; that person you met over drinks while waiting for your plane at the airport. Basically, you are instructed to make a list of everyone you know (1) who might or might not remember who you are,

(2) who are still breathing, and (3) who are capable of having a semi-coherent conversation on the phone

That is a large part of your target market as defined by the MLM companies. Unfortunately, as was discussed in previous chapters, there are virtually no products or services, other than perhaps toilet paper, that <u>everyone</u> needs. Thus, while it might look like you have a huge list of people to call, the truth is, most of them will <u>not</u> be a viable prospect for what you are selling.

By the way, did I mention the national DO NOT CALL REGISTRY? According to the rules of this government-maintained Registry, a business may not call a person at home whose name and telephone number is on the Do Not Call Registry list unless that person has "*been a customer during the last 18 months*". (There are a few exceptions including charities and political fund-raising, but nothing that is relevant to your potential MLM business.)

Note, the wording is '*has been a <u>customer</u>*'; not a friend, family member, past girlfriend, casual acquaintance, or worst enemy. As a point of legality, as an 'independent sales rep,' you will own and operate a 'business' and are, therefore, technically and legally subject to the rules that all businesses must follow related to the Do Not Call Registry.

Thus, before you call any of your friends, family and business acquaintances at their home, you should technically (and to be totally legal) run their phone numbers against the Do Not Call Registry. If their home number is on the list, you shouldn't call them at home.

<u>To be safe and legal, you should only call people at their place of business where the Do Not Call rules do not apply.</u>

Rules aside, the point I am trying to make here is that, in general, NOBODY likes to get telemarketing calls of any kind, be it from a business in town, in another state or country, or from a friend or relative.

How do you feel when someone calls you and says: "*I just started a new business and I would like you to attend a home party/event/meeting so you can learn about it.*" Be honest. You don't like it much, do you?

Yet, after you get done calling your family, friends and co-workers at work (who might buy out of guilt or just to help you out -- once), you will then have to make future sales calls to total strangers (also at their place of work).

These total strangers are likely to respond to your calls in exactly the same way you respond to such calls (by hanging up and making a mental note not to ever do business with you). Thus, one of the key ways of advertising your product or service (warm and cold calling) that was used with good effectiveness in the past is no longer nearly as effective or available as it used to be.

The point of this chapter was to bring to your attention that it isn't easy or legal in many cases to call someone up on the phone to tell them about your MLM business. Even when it is legal, it's effectiveness for promoting an MLM business has been severely impacted. You might find that networking at meetings and business associations and groups is the more effective way to get yourself in front of prospects.

Chapter 20
Suggestions on making effective presentations

If you have determined that you have the characteristics needed to have a good chance of succeeding in an MLM business, you should focus your efforts on presenting your product or service in the best way possible. There are many types of presentations that one of your prospects might attend. This chapter discusses some of the different types of presentations and makes suggestions on which kind of presentation should be made to which kind of prospect. It also offers suggestions on the most effective ways for you to present based on the kind of person you are.

Public Events

Many MLM companies offer sales presentations to which the public can be invited. Instead of having to make a sales presentation yourself, you can bring your prospect to one of these 'city-wide' events where some of the more experienced and higher-level reps will make 'professional' presentations.

These presentations are often held in hotel meeting rooms or in restaurant rooms that have been rented for this specific purpose. At some events, especially those held at restaurants, the events are often scheduled around lunch or dinner time so that the prospects (and reps) can eat a meal (which you might be expected to buy for your prospect -- another expense).

There are a number of advantages to these types of presentations. The first advantage is, if you are not a natural salesperson, or if you feel uncomfortable making presentations to more than one or two people, you can bring your prospects to these meetings, pay a fee which helps pay for the room costs, and then sit back and let one of the more seasoned reps do the presenting.

If the MLM Company has prepared sales and promotional materials, PowerPoint presentations, or videos, these will often be shown at these 'public' events. Thus, if you can bring prospects to these events, you won't need to invest in a computer, projector, screen and speakers. These items can require an investment of $2,000 - $5,000. Having someone else make that investment saves you the expense of buying them yourself.

Another advantage of these events is that it is usually easier to generate excitement in a group of 20, 50, or 100 people than it is in a group of 5-10. Thus, the more reps who bring their prospects to these events, the bigger the crowds and the more excitement that can be built (assuming, of course, that the presenter knows how to 'work-the-crowd').

MLM -- Is Multi-Level Marketing Right for You?

Most people who get into an MLM join for emotional reasons. They want to escape their humdrum lives, work less, make more, see the world, make a lot of money, and have more freedom. That is the 'hope' that is sold at these presentations. The MLM companies will often have spent significant amounts of money having professional videos made to feed the emotions of the prospects and to build their excitement to the point where -- the prospect will be anxious to sign-up. Showing these videos on big screens with loud music helps build the excitement.

Depending on the MLM Company you select and how long it has been operating in your local market area, these events might be held once every couple of weeks, once a week, or many times a week. Thus, your opportunity to take your prospects to these events will vary from market to market. If you dislike presenting yourself, you will want to coincide your prospecting calls with the schedule of these city-wide events.

One problem that happens at these events is that some of the presenters aren't very good. Many MLM companies will limit presenters to people who have reached a certain level in the company such as 'Director' or 'Silver Level' and above. Unfortunately, just because a person has reached that level does not automatically make him/her into a great presenter.

I have seen many people present who are just plain lousy at it. Being a professional and effective presenter is not something you can learn in a couple of attempts. The 'professional' presenters you will see at the regional and national MLM events have been coached, trained, and have practiced a lot to become effective presenters. If you go to a local event and the presenter is about as energizing as a brick, you shouldn't take your prospects to any recruiting events where that person will be presenting.

A mistake many people make when they first start doing presentations is that they try to present in exactly the same way that the top income earners present at events. New reps will often try to emulate the style, voice, tone, inflection, and body language of the more professionally trained presenters. New reps will also try to tell the same exact stories as the more seasoned presenters. Unfortunately, these 'mimicking' presentations often come across as forced, un-natural, boring, and amateurish.

When you present, be it to one person over coffee at Starbucks or in front of 100 people in a hotel meeting room, the first rule to remember is "<u>Be Yourself</u>." You can't be another person, so don't even try. Stay within your own style. Tell your own stories.

And for heavens sake, practice. Being an effective speaker takes practice just like anything else. The more you practice, the more comfortable and natural you will be. That is what people in the audience will really respond to.

Getting back to bringing prospects to these public events, you might want to attend a few of these events to get a feel for the quality of the different presenters before you bring your prime prospects to an event. Watch the events schedule and see who is presenting, where, and when. Then schedule your prospects to come accordingly.

I also recommend that you consider what kind of person your prospect is before you decide how he/she should be presented to. For example, if your prospect is an extroverted, natural salesperson-type, they might get excited at these large events and, thus, might be more prone to signing.

On the other hand, if your prospect is more of an introvert and not a natural sales-type, these events have the potential to overwhelm the prospect and to potentially turn him/her off.

The truth is, as I have stated in other chapters, introverted, non-sales-oriented people probably shouldn't get into an MLM business at all. But, if they do, they should make their decisions based on logical information, not based on the emotions of the moment.

Let me address one other issue about these 'mass presentations.' One of statements that you will hear made by the more 'rah-rah-oriented' company reps after mass presentations will go something like this: "*Look how successful this event was! WOW! We had over a 100 people in the room and many signed up. John/Mary/Bill/Sue (pick one) is a great presenter.*"

Unfortunately, most of this is hype. First off, at most recruiting events, over half of the people in the room will be reps who are already in the company. Thus, out of "*a hundred people in the room*", it is likely that only 40 of them are 'non-reps'. (Remember, many reps attend these meetings for social and motivational reasons even when they don't have prospects to bring to the meeting. That is why there will often be more reps at a meeting than prospects.)

In addition, you will often see a husband/wife 'prospect' couple attending these meetings together. These couples do not count as two prospects. Only one is likely to join, if at all. Thus, if there are 15 couples among the attendees, these 30 people equate to only 15 prospects.

Thus, out of the 100 people in the room we are now down to about 25 actual prospects: 10 singles and 15 couples. Now, that's not necessarily bad. Nevertheless, it is important to recognize that there were actually only 25 prospects in the room, not 100.

One of things you might want to do at these events (especially before you start bringing prospects) is to stick around after the meeting and watch to see how many prospects actually signup. It's easy to tell who is signing and who isn't. The ones who are still sitting (they haven't left) and who are working with a rep either at a computer or over some papers are actually signing up.

What you are likely to see is that only a handful of prospects will actually sign up. Let's assume that five signed on. That means that out of 25 actual prospects, only five signed up. That is a closing ratio of 20%.

Why am I telling you about this? Because the higher-level people in the company will want you to believe that the best presenters are closing 40%, 50%, or maybe even 70% or more of the prospects in the audience.

It just isn't true. And, unfortunately, this kind of hype can have a potentially negative impact on new reps. What happens is this. When a new rep only closes one out of five people to whom he/she presents (which is also equal to 20%), that rep might end up feeling that he/she is a lousy sales person and a complete failure for not having closed 40-70% of his/her prospects.

Don't let yourself get fooled by all the hype about how great some of the presenters are. Even the most effective presenters will seldom close 20% of the prospects. And, there will be lots of events at which fewer than 5% of the prospects signup on the spot.

Thus, when you are picking which events and which presenters you are going to have your prospects watch, pick those presenters who get a good percentage of prospects to sign. Some presenters are 'slick' but they don't close many prospects. Other presenters may seem less polished, but they are sometimes more effective at grabbing the prospects' emotions. Those are the prospects who are mostly likely to sign.

Home Parties

If you are as old as I am, you might remember back when 'Tupperware Parties' were all the rage. The 'Tupperware Rep' would have a woman gather a bunch of her friends together at her house and the Rep would then present all the fabulous Tupperware products to the attendees (and would, of course, take orders from anyone who wanted to buy!)

These home parties are still used as sales/recruiting events by MLM reps. Instead of renting a hotel room or restaurant (which costs money), one rep volunteers to use his/her home as the meeting place for one of these home party presentations. Perhaps half a dozen reps will get together, organize the event, arrange for some food and drink, and bring their prospects to the party.

There are a number of reasons why these types of events are held. The first, which I already mentioned, is that it is usually cheaper to do these events in someone's home versus renting a hotel or restaurant room.

A second reason is that it is supposedly easier to get a prospect to come to a 'party' at someone's home, than it is to come to an 'event' at a hotel. Calling it a party makes it sound like it is just for fun. In fact, the intent is to hide that there will be a business presentation made at the party.

(Personally, I found this 'hiding of the truth' to be distasteful and unethical. In the two MLM's in which I participated while doing research for this book, I could not bring myself to 'hide the truth' from prospects about the real purpose of the party. But, that's just my personal ethics. You will have to do what feels right to you.)

Anyway, the purpose of these parties is the same as the events at hotels: get as many prospects together as will comfortably fit in the house; have someone make the 'Company' presentation to the group; and then signup as many people as possible.

There are a number of problems that can occur at these home parties that many new reps experience the hard way. First, getting everyone comfortably situated in a room in the home so everyone can see the presentation is often a challenge. There is usually lots of furniture moving, rearranging of chairs and tables, and people sitting on the floor. (If you do one of these home parties at your home, remember to get a couple of the other reps to help you move all the furniture back after the party is over!)

Secondly, at many of these home parties, I saw: (1) kids running around, tripping over computer wires, bumping into screens, and interrupting Mommy/Daddy during the middle of the presentation, etc.; (2) dogs doing the same thing as the kids mentioned above; (3) clumsy (and occasionally drunk) adults doing the same things as the kids and dogs; (4) homes that weren't air-conditioned so that 30 people were crowded closely together in a room where the temperature was 90+ degrees.

Obviously, these things are not conducive to making an effective presentation. Thus, if you are going to hold or participate in a home party, you might want to make sure that these distractions are minimized or eliminated as much as possible.

Another drawback to advertising these events as a 'party' is that people think they can show up at a party at <u>any</u> time that suits their needs. If you tell people (the prospects) that the party starts at 6:00 p.m., some prospects will show up at 6:00; some will show at 6:30; some will arrive at 7:00; and some will arrive 'fashionably late' at 8:00. This makes it hard to decide when to start the 'presentation'. (Note that these parties are held mostly in the evening or on weekends and that food and drink are usually provided -- another expense.)

Do you start the party at 6:00 p.m. with the intention to begin the actual presentation at 7:00 p.m.? And do you start the presentation over when someone arrives at 7:20 p.m.? If not, will those who arrive late understand the information you are trying to present when they didn't hear the presentation from the beginning? Problems, problems and more problems.

Also, please take special note of the fact that if you hold a business event in your home, your homeowners' insurance is unlikely to cover liabilities (someone tripping on the power cord and breaking an arm), damage to business equipment, damage to people's cars in the driveway, etc. Thus, before you host a party at your home, check with your insurance agent to see if you need additional business insurance coverage.

If you invite prospects to a home party, you also want to think about what kind of person will find this environment acceptable. Introverts can find themselves in a totally uncomfortable situation having to interact with a bunch of strangers in close quarters. Thus, it is best to invite the party-going types to these parties, and work with the quieter types in a different setting.

One-on-One Selling

That brings us to the last of the major ways to present your MLM business to a prospect. This is where you are meeting one-on-one with a prospect. (For purposes of this section, we will also define a married couple -- or those with significant others -- as one prospect.)

For many MLM reps, especially those who are not natural sales-types, this is the most comfortable and often the most effective way to sell your product or service, as well as a comfortable way to recruit prospects for your team.

Presenting your information in this manner is far more controllable in terms of timing, location, and eliminating distractions, and allows for a much more personal interaction. For reps who are more introverted, this is probably the best option if you don't want to take them to the public events.

It is the most desirable environment for your prospects who are the quieter, more introverted types, and for those who also aren't natural sales-people. This is true for a couple of reasons.

First, these types of prospects (the quiet ones) will feel more comfortable not having to be around a bunch of 'go-getters' whom they are likely to encounter in the public events and house parties.

Secondly, if you are not a natural sales-type yourself, you, too, will feel more comfortable in this more subdued setting. (If you are an extrovert and sales-oriented, this setting won't make any difference to you one way or the other. But, it is better for the more reserved prospect.)

Finally, for the less-aggressive kind of prospects, seeing you make your presentation to them in this kind of environment will give them confidence that they, too, might be able to present to others this way. These more introverted types are unlikely to ever feel comfortable in the public events and home party settings. Nevertheless, if they are attracted to what you have to offer in this one-on-one form of presentation, they are more likely to believe that they could sell this way, too.

Thus, whether you personally are extroverted or introverted isn't the issue. You should think about what kind of presentation will be most likely to have the desired affect on your prospect.

If you are more introverted and your prospect is, too, the face-to-face, one-on-one form of presentation in a more quiet setting is the best option.

If you are introverted but your prospect is an extrovert, take him/her to one of the meetings at a hotel or restaurant where the prospect can enjoy the excitement of the crowd while you can stay in the background while one of the more senior reps makes the presentation.

If you and your prospect are both extroverted, you can take him/her to either the public events or to home parties. You will both be comfortable in either of these settings.

Remember, it is important to be yourself no matter whether you are reserved or more outgoing. Trying to pretend that you are someone other than who you naturally are will come across artificial, un-natural, and phony. Pick the kind of presentation that best fits your needs and a setting for the presentation that will make your prospect the most comfortable

As I mentioned in the section about public meetings, too often, new reps in MLM companies try to act like one of the professional presenters when they present themselves. They mimic the words, actions and stories of the more seasoned presenter.

I would suggest that you do your presentations in your own style. Pick the setting (public meeting, home party, one-on-one) that best fits who you naturally are.

Then, when you present, use the company-supplied materials and videos as much as possible. The MLM Company spent a lot of time and money having these materials done professionally so as to get the maximum affect. Why not use them and let them sell the benefits of the company?

Then, supplement the company supplied materials (when you are allowed to) with your own experiences and stories as it relates to having your own MLM business. You know your own stories well and you will deliver them more naturally and confidently than trying to tell someone else's stories.

Above all, be yourself. Don't let people convince you to present in a style that doesn't fit who you are. Figure out what feels best to you and then practice, practice, practice.

There is a quote that says "*Practice makes perfect.*" Forget about trying to be perfect as a presenter or salesperson. Strive instead for excellence. And, do it in your own style.

People trust people who are natural and who can look them in the eye. Practice until you can be comfortable with what you want to say, and then, look the prospect in the eye. In that way, you have the best chance of having your prospect listen and understand what you have to say.

Chapter 21
Recruiting from
the 'Warm Leads List'

The vast majority of money in an MLM business is made by building a big team under you. Selling the actual product or service is not where the real money is. The big earners have huge teams, sometimes with thousands of people under them in the multi-level hierarchy.

What most people don't understand is that team building in an MLM business happens primarily where the 'warm leads' are the hottest. But, what exactly does that mean?

The list of 100 or 250 or 500 people that you will be instructed to build comprises your 'warm leads list' of prospects. Why are they considered 'warm?' Because you already have some kind of relationship with those people. They already know you in some way. Because you have had some previous contact with them, even if that contact was brief, your calls to them will not be 'cold calls' to total strangers.

The rapid building of teams occurs from the 'warm leads lists' of the latest people to join the company.

Once a person has exhausted his/her warm leads, they are left with making -- cold calls. And, as I mentioned before, <u>NOBODY likes to make cold calls, or to receive them</u>.

So, once you personally recruit and sign-up as many of your warm leads as you can, you should then help your new recruits (who are now in your 'down-line') to build their list of 'warm leads' and help them go after them.

Each new group of recruits is instructed to build a warm leads list, and then the people above them help them to put on recruitment parties and events at which the next level of recruits is signed-up. The process repeats itself until there are no more new recruits with a warm leads list. It is at this point that the company starts to reach saturation in any given market.

Remember, the major portion of new recruits come from the warm leads list. These are the lowest hanging fruit for the new rep. They will mostly be family, friends, and co-workers of the new recruit.

Another important point to note is that you shouldn't waste time trying to help people in the middle or top-levels of your teams unless they are proven, natural born sales-types. Even the fairly successful people at the top and middle of your teams will have exhausted their personal warm leads lists a long time ago. And now, they have to cold call to get new leads just like everyone else who has exhausted their warm leads list. (And we all know how much fun and how productive 'cold calling' is, right? NOT!)

Work at the lowest level of your teams and keep generating the next level from the lowest level's warm leads. If you run out of warm leads, that's when things get tough. To be honest, most people run out of warm leads on their teams in a matter of weeks or months. And that is why few people ever make the big money. If you don't get into an MLM early on, it becomes increasingly harder to continue to find new prospects for the process.

Another group of targets upon whom you should focus your efforts is in identifying and recruiting natural born salespeople. Don't waste time with introverts and people who are quiet and reserved no matter how 'nice' they might be. The only way to make big money is to find the natural sales-types.

These natural salespeople at least have the possibility of knowing other natural sales-types (remember, birds of a feather, flock together.) The more natural salespeople you get onto your teams, the better the chance you will have to (1) build a workable, profitable team, and (2) the greater your chances are to stumble across a super-salesperson. You are unlikely to find super-salespeople in the slow lane of life. The more you can mix with the fast crowd, the better your chances are to find the person(s) who can take you to the big money.

Think of the target market for the particular MLM product or service you are selling like it was a fruit tree. At the bottom of the tree is what is often called the 'low-hanging fruit.' These are the people in the target market who are easiest to reach and sell. They are also the ones that are likely to have already have been 'picked' or recruited by the people who got into the MLM early.

As each new group of recruits (level) joins the company, they have to climb higher and higher into the tree to find fruit. Eventually, the top of the tree is reached and there is no more fruit (people in the target market) to pick or recruit. By this time, most of the big money earners will have either retired wealthy, or cashed out and moved on to start again in the next MLM tree, one which was most likely 'planted' by one of their friends.

There is one more thing to recognize about your personal warm leads list. If you are getting into an MLM after it has been around for a while, you are likely to find that a lot, if not most, of the people on your warm leads list will have already been contacted by other reps in either the same MLM Company, or by reps for other MLM companies.

It is estimated that eight out of every ten people over the age of 25 have either: (1) been in (and usually had a bad experience with) an MLM business; (2) has a friend or family member in an MLM business; or (3) has been contacted by someone promoting an MLM business.

The point is, most of the people on your warm leads list will not be a viable target for the product or service, and will already have a personal view of MLM companies, most of which will be negative. Therefore, don't be surprised when that huge list of 500 people you have on your warm leads list quickly narrows down to only a handful of real prospects.

So what is the point of this chapter? The point is, if you want to make money selling the actual product or service offered by the MLM, that is fine. You would probably do best by picking an MLM that has a broad product range so that you have many different consumable products to sell to different target markets.

Nevertheless, if you want to make big money, you will have to build a big team under you. Is that possible? Yes, if you meet the characteristics of a person who is good at selling (Chapter 3), and if the people you know who are on your 'warm list' are <u>also</u> people who are extroverted salespeople.

If, on the other hand, you don't know many people who are natural born salespeople whom you can recruit onto your team, you are unlikely to build a big team from your 'warm leads list' alone. And, once you have exhausted your warm leads list and the warm leads lists of the few people you recruited under you, you will have to start selling the old fashioned way, by making ----- cold calls and networking! If that is something you like doing, go for it. Just don't expect to make much money from it.

At this point, you might want to rethink how much you can/will make in the particular MLM business you are in. Recruiting teams is where the big money is made but it is also the hardest thing to do as you move higher in the tree.

The Top Income Earners benefit no matter who makes the sale. But each successive level of reps has fewer opportunities to make it big. (If you think about the fruit tree analogy, remember that the smaller and smaller amounts of unpicked, ripe fruit remaining higher in the tree will always tumble down to the big income earners with the huge teams. But, there is never any unpicked fruit at the lower levels that will rise up to the reps above!)

If you are still thinking about getting into an MLM and you want to build a huge team so you can make big bucks, get into the MLM tree as early as you can, preferably before the official launch of the product/service. Then, work as hard and as fast as you can to recruit super-salespeople under you who will continue to push the levels below them, helping the newest recruits to aggressively go after each successive list of warm leads. That is the best way to build big teams and make big money.

Chapter 22
The 'Luck Factor'
in recruiting

If you talk to the people who are making the most money in MLM businesses, you will find that most have those characteristics that I have previously mentioned: (1) successful in a previous business; (2) natural born sales-people; (3) outgoing, Type A, extroverts who like being around people; (4) got in early in the MLM business, probably before it was officially launched.

But, occasionally you will come across a person who doesn't seem to meet those criteria. You will encounter the occasional money earner who seems quiet, reserved, not at all out-going. The person is not a celebrity nor were they particularly successful in business before getting into their MLM business.

I was curious as to how and why these people had become successful in an MLM even though they didn't possess many of the requisite characteristics that would have aided their success.

After doing some research and talking to some of these individuals and members of their teams, one critical factor came to light. What is that factor?

A few of the big money earners had simply been <u>lucky</u> in recruiting a couple of superstars onto their teams.

There is an old gambler's adage which says: "*I'd rather be lucky than good.*" It is hard to argue with this idea, and it is the best explanation of why a tiny percentage of people make some good money from an MLM even though they really don't fit the mold of a big-money earner.

The question is, is there anything that can be learned from this 'luck factor' to help you become a big money-earner, too? Yes, there is.

The secret (actually, it isn't really a 'secret' -- it's more of a logical deduction) to building big teams is to dedicate much of your recruiting time and efforts to finding and recruiting 'super-salespeople.'

'Super-Salespeople' are those rare people who are natural born salespeople, and who also happen to be successful business owners or managers who are at a crossroads in their lives where they are looking for a new challenge.

I know of a few people who are making decent money from an MLM business who were lucky enough to recruit a couple of these super-salespeople onto their teams. (By the way, it is generally easiest to make money in an MLM Comp Plan known as the Binary Plan where you have only two teams below you. If you get into an

MLM -- Is Multi-Level Marketing Right for You?

MLM with a Comp Plan with three or four or more 'legs', you will likely have to recruit a super-salesperson for every 'leg' of your team. Thus, it is much easier to find and recruit two super-salespeople for a binary plan, than it is to have to find and recruit three, four or more super-salespeople for plans with multiple legs to support.)

Among the people who are making serious money, it is interesting to note that they seldom personally recruited more than a handful of the people on their teams. Yet, they sometimes end up with thousands of people on their teams. Obviously, this didn't happen because they were good at recruiting. In actuality, they were simply <u>lucky</u> enough to have recruited a couple of super-salespeople, and those super-salespeople <u>were</u> GREAT at recruiting others like themselves.

So, what does this mean to you? If you recognize that you are not a person who possesses many of the characteristics that will make you a great salesperson and recruiter, your best hope of making decent money is to find a couple of super-salespeople and to get them on the different 'legs' of your team.

How do you find and recruit these super-salespeople? Beats the heck out of me. Hey, if I knew how to do that, wouldn't I have done it and be sitting on the beach sipping Pina Coladas while my super-salespeople went out and tore up the world?

Of course I would have. So, sorry to disappoint you but, I don't know a 'secret' way to find, identify, and recruit these people. And, best as I can determine, neither does anyone else. Not even the Top Income Earners talk of a <u>consistent</u> and proven way to meet and recruit these kinds of people.

That is why I said that the people who got these type of super-salespeople on their teams were just plain <u>lucky</u>.

Nevertheless, you should <u>always</u> be on the lookout for these super-sales-types. You might also take into consideration that you are unlikely to find a super-salesperson among the people you already know. If you are not a natural born salesperson and a successful business owner, the people you know are unlikely to have come from the super-salesperson mold. Thus, it is highly unlikely that you will find a super-salesperson on your warm leads list.

That means that you will have to look elsewhere. Where? Anywhere. Everywhere. Nowhere. Somewhere. These super-salespeople are 'out there', but they are harder to find and recruit than looking for a six-leaf clover.

That doesn't mean that you won't find one. Just be aware that placing your hopes of making big money in an MLM on finding a couple of super-salespeople is like betting on the lottery -- someone will win, but millions won't.

Chapter 23
When you 'Recruit' someone onto your MLM 'Team', they become a direct competitor

One of the big differences between doing direct sales of a product or service and being in an MLM business is that in an MLM business, the big money is made from commissions and bonuses you receive for recruiting people onto your 'team'. If you investigate most MLM businesses, the big money makers make little money from the actual sale of the product or service to regular consumers. Retail sales to non-members of the MLM are minimal.

Why is this important? Because, when you stop and think about it, <u>when you recruit someone to be on your team, you are bringing in someone who will be a direct competitor of yours to sell the actual product or service in the marketplace, and to recruit new members for THEIR team.</u>

Most business owners, the ones who have regular, non-MLM-types of businesses, would prefer to have a monopoly on any product or service they are selling. The fewer competitors they have, the more sales that leaves for them.

But, this is not the case in an MLM business. When you think about it, if you want to be able to sell a lot of the actual product or service in your market area, recruiting as many direct competitors as possible is totally illogical.

Would you rather sell vitamins or jewelry or cosmetics (or anything) in a market area that has two competitors, or 2,000? Seems like an easy question to answer, doesn't it? Yet, in an MLM business, you will make the most money by signing up as many competitors as possible.

Now, you might say that it doesn't matter if there are other competitors if no one is selling the actual product. To some extent that is true. But, again, it is not from selling the actual product or service that you are going to get rich (or even make much of a basic income). Recruiting is the key.

But if recruiting is the key, this raises a couple more questions. (1) What is the best way to recruit? (2) Doesn't it become harder and harder to make money from recruiting new people as more and more competitors join in? (Remember, every new rep also hopes and wants to make BIG money, too. The only way to do that is for them to be actively recruiting in the same market area you are.)

Think about it this way. Would you prefer to recruit in a market area where there are only two other people recruiting, or 2,000? The logical answer seems clear. The more reps there are in the local area, the more reps there are trying to sell to the same people in the area in which you are trying to recruit members for your team.

MLM -- Is Multi-Level Marketing Right for You?

At some point, any given market area is going to reach a saturation point, the point at which there are no more people to recruit who haven't already been approached. That is why you have your best chance of succeeding in an MLM if you get in right at the launch of the company.

Now, the MLM companies will confidently state that there is no such thing as 'saturating' a market. They will tell you that there are always more people who haven't been approached for the particular product or service being sold by their MLM Company.

Think about that logically for a moment. In a town or city of any given size, do you think that there is an unlimited market for <u>any</u> product or service that isn't being provided by a number of other companies with similar products? Highly unlikely. Think back to the vitamin example in Anywhere, USA.

Of course, from an MLM company's perspective, the more reps they have, the more money the top earners in the company will make. But, in the vast majority of cases, those top earners are not making money from the actual sales of products or services to the general public. They are making money only because people keep joining their MLM teams in hopes that they, too, can make big money in an MLM business.

Even if some product sales are being made, the more reps there are, the more the sales (and the remaining potential recruits) are being divvied up among more and more people. The more reps there are, the less each rep is likely to make in commissions from actual product sales and the fewer potential recruits there are that are left to be acquired.

The point of this chapter is to make sure that you have a clear understanding of the potential for making money selling the actual MLM product or service to consumers, versus the potential money to be made by recruiting more members onto your team. The higher the level you enter into the tree of an MLM business, the less fruit there is to pick and the more people there are who are trying to pick it. This, unfortunately, results in a lot of people with empty baskets.

Nevertheless, if you decide you want to make some real money from an MLM business, you'd better learn how to recruit people effectively and efficiently. I'll address that issue further in the next chapter.

Chapter 24
How the 80/20 Rule applies to an MLM business

Have you ever heard of the 80/20 Rule? Many people have. But, even for those who have heard of it, many people don't understand it or have a good idea of how it can help you run your MLM business (and your life).

In a 2008 study of MLM companies called "*The Myth of "Income Opportunity" in Multi-Level Marketing*" by Robert L. Fitzpatrick, the author shows that in most MLM companies, 1% of the reps receive 50% or more of the total commissions. Those numbers might seem outrageous. Nevertheless, it is interesting that these numbers are almost predictable when one looks at the 80/20 rule.

The 80/20 Rule

Vilfredo Pareto was born in Italy in 1848. He was one of the leaders of the Lausanne School, a group whose ideas have guided much of economics ever since. Pareto's 'rule' states that for many phenomena, 20% of invested input is responsible for 80% of the results obtained. Put another way, 80% of consequences stem from 20% of the causes. Pareto constructed the rule as a way to explain why only 20% of the population in Italy at that time owned 80% of the property.

Please note that the 80/20 Rule (also known as Pareto's Law) is not a mathematically proven or derived rule. It is just one of those interesting facts that seems to apply to lots of things in the world.

What is important for you to understand is that, in many instances, we find that a small percentage of one thing accounts for a significantly higher percentage of something else to which it is related.

For example, if you look in your closet, you are likely to find that you wear 20% of your clothes 80% of the time. Of all the restaurants you go to, you tend to go to just 20% of them 80% of the time. And, of all the entrees on the menu, you will order 20% of them 80% of the time.

Thus, this interesting phenomenon applies to many things in the world. And, it is useful to understand how it might apply to your MLM business.

It is not mandatory or likely that the percentages will always be exactly 80% and 20%. The actual numbers might be 65% and 27%, or 70% and 22%. The numbers could just as easily go the other way, too, whereby the percentages might be 83% and 15% (you wear 15% of your clothes 83% of the time).

In business, a couple of quick examples would include: 20% of a corporation's staff might be responsible for 80% of the firm's profits; 20% of your customers might account for 80% of your profits; 20% of your products may account for 80% of sales. And, on the negative side, 20% of your customers will likely account for 80% of the complaints and problems.

As it relates to the number of reps in an MLM and the amount of commissions they receive, the 80/20 rule would predict that 20% of the reps in an MLM Company would account for 80% of the total commissions. This is not far from the actual numbers for many MLM's.

What few people know about the 80/20 rule is that the rule can be applied to itself. Let me give an example to explain what this means and how it applies to MLM commissions.

Suppose we had an MLM company that had 100,000 reps and those reps received total commissions of $10,000,000. This works out to an 'average' commission of $100 (which, unfortunately, is often not far from the truth.)

The 80/20 rule predicts that 20,000 of the 100,000 reps (20%) will account for $8,000,000 of the total $10,000,000 of commissions (80%).(Table 6)

Table 6

	Reps	% of Reps	Commis- sions	% of Comm.
Totals	100,000	100%	$10,000,000	100%
Top 20%	20,000	20%	$8,000,000	80%
Bottom 80%	80,000	80%	$2,000,000	20%

Now, here is where the application of the 80/20 rule can get interesting. Somewhere out in the world there is another MLM company that has 20,000 total reps who receive total commissions of $8,000,000. For this company, the 80/20 rule would predict that only 4,000 reps (20% of the total 20,000 reps) will account for $6,400,000 of the total commissions (80% of $8,000,000 = $6,400,000). (Table 7)

Table 7

	Reps	% of Reps	Commis-sions	% of Comm.
Totals	20,000	100%	$8,000,000	100%
Top 20%	4,000	20%	$6,400,000	80%
Bottom 80%	16,000	80%	$1,600,000	20%

But, we're not done yet. Out in the world there is yet another MLM company which has a total of 4,000 reps who receive $6,400,000 in total commissions. For this company, the 80/20 rule would predict that 800 reps (20% of the total 4,000 reps) will receive $5,120,000 of the total commissions (80% of $6,400,000 = $5,120,000). (Table 8)

Table 8

	Reps	% of Reps	Commis-sions	% of Comm.
Totals	4,000	100%	$6,400,000	100%
Top 20%	800	20%	$5,120,000	80%
Bottom 80%	3,200	80%	$1,280,000	20%

Actually, these three companies are the same company. When I said that the 80/20 rule can be applied to itself, it means that within the group of 20,000 reps who represent $8,000,000 of total commissions, there is a subgroup of only 4,000 who are getting $6,400,000 of the total commissions. And further, <u>within the group of 4,000 reps, there is an even smaller subgroup of only 800</u> who will receive $5,120,000 of the total commissions. (Table 9)

Table 9

	Reps	% of Reps	$ Comm.	% of Comm.
Totals	100,000	100%	$10,000,000	100%
Top 20%	20,000	20%	$8,000,000	80%
Best 20% of Top 20%	4,000	4%	$6,400,000	64%
Best of the Best of Best	800	0.8%	$5,120,000	51.2%

So, what do these numbers say when we get right down to it? They show that the 80/20 rule would predict that only 800 of the very, very, very best reps, or less than 1% of the total 100,000 reps, are likely to receive 51.2% of the total commissions ($5,120,000).

Remember when I stated at the start of this chapter the study that said that many MLM companies report that 1% of the reps account for 50% of the commissions? Well, the 80/20 rule predicts that this would be true. Scary, isn't it?

Now, there is one other prediction the 80/20 rule would make about the distribution of commissions among the 100,000 reps. (I'm not going to confuse you with more calculations; just accept that what I am saying can be shown using the 80/20 rule.)

The 80/20 rule also predicts that the Top 36% percent of reps (about one-third) will receive 96% of the total commissions ($9,600,000). If that is true (and these numbers prove to be amazing close for many MLM's based on the numbers they make available), this also means that <u>the bottom 64% of reps (approximately two-thirds) will receive only 4% of the total commissions</u> ($400,000)!

This means that the Top 36% of reps in the example company can expect to make an annual average commission of $266 each. The bottom two-thirds of the company's reps can expect to make an average of --- $6.25 --- per year! (Table 10)

Table 10

	Number of Reps	Total Commissions	Average Annual Comm.
Top ~0.8%	800	$5,120,000	$6,400
Top 20%	20,000	$8,000,000	$400
Top 36%	36,000	$9,600,000	$267
Bottom 64%	64,000	$400,000	$6.25

Now, I hear you saying that this can't possibly be true. But, unfortunately, it is. If you don't believe it, ask for the numbers from the MLM Company you are thinking of joining. But, don't be surprised if they won't give you the numbers. And, don't be surprised if the numbers come amazingly close to these predictions if you do get the numbers from some of the companies.

The question is, how can you use this 80/20 rule to help you make your MLM business more effective and profitable?

The way to use this is to understand that even among your own team members (the people you have recruited below you on your team), these same percentages and distributions are likely to occur.

Thus, if you have 100 reps on your team, it is likely that 1% of them (one rep) will end up being responsible for 50% of the money you make from your team (does the word 'super-salesperson come to mind?)

On your team, 20 reps (20%) will account for 80% of your revenue. And, 36 of the reps on your team (36%) are likely to be responsible for 96% of your income!

So, let me ask you this question. If you have only a limited amount of time available to help the 100 reps on your team build their teams, do you want to allocate that limited time to the 64 reps on your team who account for only 4% of your revenue, or to the 36 reps who will be responsible for 96% of your commissions?

Further, within the 36 reps who will account for 96% of your income, do you want to allocate most of your time to the 1 rep who will account for 50% of your business, to the 4 reps who will account for 64% of your business, to the 20 reps who will account for 80%, or will you equally distribute your time across all 36 reps?

It seems logical to me that you would want to allocate whatever time you have available to help those reps who account for the biggest percentage of your commissions.

As you build your teams, pay close attention to which reps are the natural born salespeople and pay special attention to the super-stars. When you identify these types, dedicate your available time to helping them build their teams.

As for the other 64 reps on your team who are going to contribute only 4% of your commissions, frankly, you shouldn't spend much time worrying about them. They will likely be gone within a year anyway, and they are unlikely to sign up many new customers no matter how much help you give them.

Chapter 25
Effective Networking

In Chapter 10, I discussed 'networking' as one of the ways to market your MLM product or service, and as a way to meet and recruit new members for your team. I want to offer some additional information on how to network more effectively, using the 80/20 Rule as a targeting tool.

NOTE: <u>The following information is for people who really want/need to make money from their MLM business. If you are in an MLM just for social reasons, then go to as many networking events as you want and have fun.</u>

As I discussed in Chapter 10, there are many business networking organizations including 'leads/referral groups', Chambers of Commerce, business organizations and associations, and other similar groups. It is unfortunate that most people do not know how to network effectively when they attend functions sponsored by these groups.

Let me use the 80/20 Rule to show how most people use their time at networking events. The 'average' person will spend 80% of his/her time at a networking event going after people in the room who are likely to provide only 20% of his/her business.

Even worse, the 'average' person will often spend 64% of his time with people who will provide only 4% of the business she will get from the networking group.

In truth, most people who attend networking events cuddle up next to people they already know so that they don't have to make cold calls on the strangers in the room. Unfortunately, in an MLM business, you are unlikely to generate much new business from people you already know and who already know about your MLM business.

When you attend a networking event, you must get it in your mind that not all the people attending the event are good prospects for your MLM product or service. If there are 100 people attending the event, 20 of them represent 'possible' targets. Four of the people in the room represent 'good' targets and only one person in the room is a 'great' target (if there are any at all).

So, you first have to commit yourself to use your time effectively to narrow down the field to 20 targets. How do you do this? You circulate quickly through the crowd, watching, listening, and using your instincts to pick out the most likely prospects.

These prospects will exhibit the characteristics of those most likely to succeed in an MLM business: (1) natural sales-types; (2) outgoing, extroverted and confident; (3) they are talking more than listening; (4) they will often talk loudly and with exaggerated movements of the hands and arms; (5) they seem to have attracted a small crowd around them.

MLM -- Is Multi-Level Marketing Right for You?

As you circulate around the room, make notes on a small notepad when you see people who meet these characteristics. Don't waste time on people who are standing by themselves, head down, acting like wallflowers who wish they were at home. These are not going to be the more aggressive sales-types you are looking to recruit for your team. Introverts are not your target, so don't waste time on them.

After you have scouted the meeting to get the 'lay of the land', start narrowing down your best targets. Remember, you are looking for four to six really good prospects. Once you have narrowed the field to this number, rank them in priority order and go after the top ranked one first.

Move into the group where this person is probably at the center. Now is not the time to be shy. If you are shy, you are not going to succeed at an MLM business. So, spit out any butterflies you may have in your stomach and move onto the field to play the game.

Do whatever is necessary to introduce yourself to your prime target. Make sure you compliment the person about something within the first minute you meet him/her. These types of people have big egos that need to be fed. Your job is to feed his/her ego and get it on your side.

Please understand that you are going to let this person talk 95% of the time while you ask questions about him/her the other 5%. During the conversation, which might be brief, make sure the person hears your name, give them your business card, and get their business card. Tell them that you would like to get together over coffee sometime to hear more about what they do.

If this person seems like a 'go-getter' who meets the criteria of a person you would like to have on your team, let them talk to you as long as they want to. Hog their time as long as they will give it to you. Remember, you are here for business, not to worry about giving all your other competitors in the room an equal shot at your potential superstar.

Eventually, someone whom your target knows will come and join in the conversation. At that point, you can politely tell your target that you enjoyed talking to him/her and that you will give him/her a call later in the week to set up a time to get together.

Then, move to a place where you can quickly make notes about the person: what he looks like; things she talked about; and any personal information you learned during the 'one-sided' conversation. You will use that information when you get together with the person over coffee or lunch.

Once you have your notes in order on Target #1, move on to Target #2 and repeat the process. If you come across a target who doesn't seem to meet your criteria (after you watch or listen to them a little as they talk to others before you move in), scratch him/her off the list and move on to Target #3.

By the way, as a general rule, do not try to 'close a sale' at a networking event. Your primary goal is to get your target to agree to talk/meet with you at a future time when you can have his/her full attention. People who try to 'sell business' at networking events come across as pushy salespeople. Remember, "*People love to buy, but they hate to be sold.*" Your objective is to identify your best targets, meet them, and to get them to agree to meet with you again at a future time.

Keep in mind that you are after quality, not quantity. You are looking for a handful of good-to-great prospects for your team. During a two-hour event, you should probably talk to no more than 10 people, of which you would like to converse with two-three of them for 20 minutes each. If you get through your first set of targets quickly, move onto the next most likely targets.

What do you do if you start a conversation with one of your targets and the person turns out to be a dud? In these situations, you will have to politely listen for a few minutes, and then you can excuse yourself to 'go to the bathroom.' You don't want to offend the person, but, you are wasting valuable time with him/her if you know they don't fit the profile of people you want on your team. So, politely excuse yourself and move on to your next target.

Here are a few more pointers to consider.

If the event is an evening 'mixer' where people are having drinks and munching on appetizers, eat and drink <u>before</u> you go so you can keep both hands free while you are talking to people. Too many people hold a drink in their hand as a crutch. In addition, fumbling around trying to balance a drink and a plate of egg rolls makes it hard to shake someone's hand, to get their business card, and to give them yours.

Also, even if you like to drink alcoholic beverages, my recommendation is that you stick to soda or water if you have anything at the event. You want to be on the top of your game if you are going to take on the 'hotshots'. Alcohol dulls your senses and responses. And, of course, getting drunk and putting a lampshade on your head is totally inappropriate. You want to come across as being intelligent, a great listener, and proficient at what you do.

If the networking event is a luncheon or breakfast at which you will eventually have to sit down at a table with only six or eight other attendees, try to sit next to your prime targets. Use the time before 'dinner is served' to scope out your targets and to strategically place yourself so that you can conveniently join them at their table.

Most people who go to networking events are primarily there to socialize, not to actually get business. But, if you want to be successful in your MLM business, or any business for that matter, you should consider these events as work time.

Remember when I said that most successful business owners work 40-60 hour weeks, especially when they are first starting the business? Well, these networking events are part of work time. Use the time effectively and do your socializing at a different time and place.

Keep the 80/20 Rule in mind as you 'work' the event. Spend the majority of your time on those prospects who have the greatest potential to make a valuable addition to your team. Otherwise, you are likely to end up being one of the 64% of MLM reps who account for only 4% of the commissions earned.

Chapter 26
Your MLM business website

As I mentioned in Chapter 10, most MLM companies provide their independent reps with a 'personal website'. The MLM companies proudly talk about how they have spent 'millions of dollars' developing the software and systems behind these sites, and that all you have to do is sign-up as a member and you will get 'your own personal website for your business that we will maintain for you' (for a fee, of course).

Wow, that sounds great, doesn't it? Your own website and you don't have to develop it or maintain it. Yes, that is good. The question you must ask, however, is: "*How much business am I going to actually generate through my site?*"

The first thing to consider is that <u>EVERY</u> independent rep for the MLM Company you join will also have his/her own personal website, one that is identical to yours. That creates a number of problems, none of which are good for generating business for you.

First, if a person somehow hears about the MLM Company you are a rep for, and goes on-line to search for that Company by name, he/she won't be taken to your website (or any of the other independent reps' personal websites). No, he will be taken to the MLM Company's home website which talks about the MLM Company. If this happens, and she wants to signup, she can usually do so right there.

If this happens, who gets credit for the sale and where are they placed in the multi-level tree? They are usually placed one of two ways: (1) They are specifically assigned to a particular person in the hierarchy, usually one of the top earners; or (2) they are assigned at random at the lowest level of the pyramid.

In Assignment Method (1) you will never get credit for one of these new customers. In Assignment Method (2) your odds of getting that person assigned under you are 1 in 100,000 or 250,000 or 1,000,000, depending on how many active reps there are in the Company. The point is, you are not likely to ever get credit for a person signed-up on the Company site.

This leads us to the next question which is: "*How would somebody actually find my personal site so that I can get credit for signing them up and for the orders they place?*"

The answer is, <u>you will have to have prior contact with them to direct them to your website.</u> That means you will have already met them face-to-face, with a 'cold telephone call' to them at their place of business, at a recruiting event, through a direct mail piece (where allowed), or perhaps at some networking meeting.

The point is, nobody is going to randomly find your website. Some MLM Companies will talk about how your personal website is like a "*twenty-four hour vending machine where the customer can buy your product and you get the commissions without doing any work.*" That will be true only <u>after</u> you have previously met them, got them to signup as a customer (either in person or on-line), and they then make future purchases through your website.

Thus, your website might be useful for signing people up and taking orders. Nevertheless, you are unlikely to generate many new customers or recruits for your team because they happened to stumble across your website, especially when you consider that your website is just one out of the 1,000's of other reps' websites for the MLM company you are in.

The second part of your website is often referred to as 'the back office'. This is where the accounting and other functions of your business are maintained. Having the accounting, paperwork, billings, collections, etc., done by the company is good in one way, and bad in another. As was previously mentioned, having the company handle the accounting leaves that time available for you to be out selling.

On the other hand, if the company handles all the accounting, how will you know if you are getting your proper commissions, bonuses, etc.? There is no ready solution to this problem other than trying to keep a separate set of books on your own and keeping track of how many customers you signup.

If customers can place their own orders without going through you, you may never know that they made additional purchases for which you should have received commissions. You will only be able to keep an accurate track of the commissions you should receive from direct sales of the product if you place the orders yourself.

In either case, determine how the accounting is done for any MLM you are considering joining. President Ronald Reagan made famous the statement: "*Trust, but verify*." It is an excellent quote to remember when determining which MLM company you will join and whether you will be able to verify what is owed to you.

Chapter 27
'Social Networking' and an MLM business

Today, social networking is all the rage. FaceBook and YouTube and Twitter are the hottest things going in the electronic culture in which we live. A question you might ask is: "*Can I use these 'electronic social networking' groups to my advantage in marketing my MLM business?*"

My answer is: I don't think so. Now, that probably is not the answer you would get from a lot of people who think these groups are low hanging fruit just waiting to be picked.

So why do I think these social networking groups are unlikely to generate much business for you? Because these groups are, by definition, <u>'Social Networking'</u> groups.

In a previous chapter I talked about various 'Business Networking Groups' that you might join such as LeTip, BNI, Chambers of Commerce, and the many types of business organizations and associations. The primary purpose of these face-to-face, business networking groups is to generate more business and referrals for all the members of the group. Thus, the purpose of the group aligns with your goals to get more business.

There are also an increasing number of 'business-oriented social networks' (let's call them BOSN's for short) materializing on the Internet. Some of the more well-known would include LinkedIn, Ecademy, Ryze and Naymz.

These BOSN's have varied purposes and audiences. Some are basically places where a person can look or be seen, especially for purposes of getting and posting jobs.

Some BOSN's are dedicated to helping small businesses get start-up funding. Some offer places for business owners to exchange ideas and suggestions on how to better run a business.

Unfortunately, despite all the visibility some of these BOSN's are generating, I find little evidence that anyone is generating many actual sales from being a participant in these groups. When you stop and think about it, this should not be a surprising finding. Why?

Because these networking groups are just an electronic version of regular business networking practices. The primary advantage they offer, if you can call it that, is that you can electronically network with anyone, anywhere, instead of only networking in your local area.

The question is, does anyone get a sudden, unfulfilled need to purchase something from some person they find on the Internet just because they are now linked to that person through an electronic business interchange? I don't think so.

If you have a business such as being a consultant or coach, or providing advertising design or website design, you might be able to find new customers by social business networking and by being 'recommended' by others in your network. But, <u>I don't think the same can be said for sales of the usual MLM products such as vitamins, jewelry, cosmetics, or even financial or legal services.</u>

Besides, there is a good likelihood that there is at least one local rep for many MLM companies in most medium-to-large cities. Why would someone want to do business with a person/rep who offers a product or service from 1,000 miles away when they can get the identical product from a local rep? Most people won't.

So, when it comes to these 'Social Networks', there is little evidence to suggest that they will offer an effective way to sell MLM products and services, or to recruit new people for your team.

There is a saying in advertising that states: "*People love to buy, but they hate to be sold.*" How true, how true. Just like the overload of spam in email systems, if these 'social business networking' sites start becoming just another way to irritate people with unwanted advertising, they will soon lose their effectiveness, even for their original purposes. This has already happened in the social networking sites that have succumbed to allowing advertising. There is little reason to think the same won't happen to the BOSN's.

The point is, you are not going to be able to rely on Business-Oriented Social Networks as an effective way to sell most MLM products and services. You are still going to have to make most of your product sales and recruit most of your new people the old fashioned way -- through persistence, hard work, and person-to-person contact.

PART 3:
Final Thoughts

Chapter 28
The nine kinds of people in MLM businesses

After having spent some time looking into MLM businesses and talking to people who are in them (or who were at one time), there are nine categories that people fall into:

(1) Have no idea what an MLM business is -- and probably never will.

(2) Considered getting into an MLM business but decided for various reasons not to join, and likely never will.

(3) Joined and became hugely successful --having the necessary characteristics

(4) Joined and became somewhat successful -- having the necessary characteristic.

(5) Joined but not successful -- having the necessary characteristics.

(6) Joined and became marginally successful -- not having the necessary characteristics.

(7) Joined but not successful -- not having the necessary characteristics

(8) Joined, not successful, got frustrated, quit; joined another MLM, not successful, got frustrated, quit; and so on. Unlikely to ever be successful no matter how many MLM's they try.

(9) Joined, got frustrated, and quit forever.

Group #1 is comprised of people who know nothing about MLM businesses even though they may know some people who are in them. For most of these people, owning and operating their own business is not something they think about doing. They are unlikely to ever get involved in an MLM business.

Group #2 is probably the largest group in the population. Many people in the U.S. know people who are in MLM's, and they have been approached to be 'recruited' into the fold. For any number of reasons (poor image of MLM's, no time, no money, happy doing what they are currently doing), these people are unlikely to join an MLM.

Group #3 are the big money earners in MLM's. They are the Top 1% who will rake in 50-70% of all commissions and bonuses. They possess most of the necessary characteristics that would make them pre-disposed to be successful in any business.

(Please note that there are an estimated 30 million people involved in MLM businesses worldwide. This is not the number of people who have ever been involved in an MLM, only the ones who are currently involved. Thus, only 300,000 people, the Top 1%, are going to make big money. That's not many people out of a world-wide population of 6.3 billion people. Each of the 300,000 Top Earners represents only one out of every 21,000,000 people. Could you be one of them?)

(Also, please note that total sales for all MLM companies are estimated to be $100 billion a year. That may sound like a lot but, if you divide $100 billion by 30,000,000 reps, the average <u>sales</u> per rep, per year are $3,333. You can guess for yourself what the average commissions are, especially after expenses.)

Group #4 is comprised of people who had many of the required characteristics to be successful in an MLM, but for numerous reasons, they have only been able to make a little money in the business.

Group #5 is made up of people who possess many of the necessary characteristics that might have given them the opportunity to be successful, but weren't. Many of these 'fast starters' got bored when things didn't happen as quickly as they would like. Thus, many of them give an MLM a try, but quickly move on to newer and more exciting opportunities when the business doesn't develop as fast as they had hoped.

Group #6 are people who, through hard work and persistence, managed to make a little money in an MLM. But they didn't have the characteristics needed to become hugely successful, and never will.

Group #7 are people who joined an MLM without possessing many of the characteristics needed to have a chance at being successful. They may work hard at the business, keep on trying, and keep hoping, but they are unlikely to ever make even a decent salary. They won't make the big money because they are ineffective at re-cruiting, and that's where the big money is made.

Group #8 are people who joined an MLM without the necessary skills that would have given them the chance to succeed. They try hard, fail miserably, quit, and then look for another MLM that will be "the right one for them this time to be able to make it big." They will continue to try and fail, becoming almost addicted to finding the next, right MLM that will help them achieve their dreams. Unfortunately, after expenses, they are unlikely to ever break even on all their MLM investments. But, they will keep on hoping and trying. They are the people the MLM's love to recruit, and unfortunately, there are quite a few of them in the world.

Group #9 are people who joined an MLM, gave it a go, got frustrated when they realized that what was adver-tised was not what they got, and quit. In their minds they were 'burned' once and they won't ever get close to an MLM 'hot stove' again.

Which kind of person are you? Are you truly one of the rare breed, that one person out of every 21 million who could make a fortune in an MLM? Maybe you are. If so, go for it. Someone wins the lotteries. Just try to make sure you have the necessary characteristics that give you the best chance to win.

If you aren't the kind of person who is a natural-born, out-going, salesperson who knows lots of other people who possess the same characteristics, you are more likely to win a lottery than to make a fortune in an MLM. But, if the cost isn't too high, and if you don't set your expecta-tions too high, go ahead and give it a go.

Chapter 29
Is Multi-Level Marketing right for you?

If you have read all the way through this book, you are probably (1) already in an MLM business and trying to figure out how to make it work; (2) looking to join for social reasons; (3) looking to join as a way to learn about running your own business; or (4) you are still considering joining an MLM as a way to fame and fortune. I hope that the information presented in this book will help you with your decision no matter what reason you have for being in an MLM.

Are MLM's for everyone? No. Are there positive benefits that a person can gain by participating in an MLM? Yes. Can <u>anyone</u> make a fortune in an MLM business? Unlikely. Can the 'average' person make a decent living in an MLM? Seldom.

Think of an MLM company like it was a professional football team. There the owners of the team, (who probably also own the stadium); there are the coaches on the team; there are the 53 players on the team, of which only 11 are on the playing field at any time; and then there are 75,000 people in the stands who bought a ticket to watch.

The owners of the team make money as long as they field a reasonably competitive team. They make money from the tickets sold, parking concessions, food and beverage sales in the stadium, and from the sale of television rights to broadcast the games to the general public.

The coaches get paid well as long as they keep the team relatively competitive.

The players get paid for playing and winning. Winners get paid more; losers are eliminated from the team.

Then there are the paying customers in the stands. They pay for tickets, parking, food and beverages, t-shirts, hats, plastic football helmets, and the pleasure of watching the game with 74,999 other fanatics (where did you think the word 'fan' came from?)

Much of this is similar to an MLM company. The MLM Company has owners that make money from ticket sales to the fans (initial investments by reps to join the company).

The owners of the MLM Company make money from the sale of food, beverages, t-shirts, and plastic helmets (jewelry, vitamins, cosmetics, travel, legal and financial services sold by the reps).

The MLM owners also make money from providing on-going 'team building and support' items such as sales materials, training, computer services, websites and accounting services, and even from occasionally providing the 'stadium' so all the fans can get together at one time (otherwise known as company conventions.)

And, of course, the more fans the team has, the more money the owners make.

MLM -- Is Multi-Level Marketing Right for You?

The MLM 'team' has a dozen coaches or so that provide training, motivation (at conventions and recruiting events), and discipline. Of course, just as on a football team, the MLM coaches never actually play in the game. They just stand on the sidelines and tell other people what to do.

The 'players' on an MLM team are the Top 1% of the reps. They are the ones who actually get to play in the real game of making money. But, just as it is on a football team, there aren't many MLM reps who actually get to play in the money-making game. And, even at this level, reps come and go if they don't continue to play at a consistently high level.

Finally, in the MLM business there are the 75,000 fans in the stands. These are all the other reps who joined the MLM Company. They pay their money to have a chance to participate in the game; but, in reality, they are really only going to be spectators who watch from the stands. They will never have the skills, experience or opportunity to play the real game that happens only on the field.

The reps in the stands of the MLM Company can have fun doing a lot of yelling and arm waving to loud music; they can revel and participate in the roar of the crowd; and they can loyally and enthusiastically support the team. But, the truth is, they will never have the chance to play on the field where the money is actually made. For the 75,000 reps, the flow of money is always out of their wallet or purse, not in.

Many reps (often after only a year with the MLM team) quickly tire of not winning at the MLM game, and they leave in search of better teams. New reps take their place with the hopes that the team will get better because of their participation, and that they will get to reap the rewards of being an enthusiastic and loyal participant.

Once the team owners have raked in a lot of money, they slowly start cutting back on expenses. The condition of the stadium starts to deteriorate. The quality of players drops off dramatically. Soon, the team is losing money and the owners either sell out, or move to another town, where they often start a new team, perhaps a basketball team this time.

They start this new MLM team in a virgin market where the fans don't know about the team's past experience of making money only for the owners, coaches and superstar players, and of bringing little real financial success to the fans in the stands (reps). The owners rely on the eagerness of the new reps in the new market to support the team through its formative years. The reps put their full faith, trust and energy behind the team with the fervent, unwavering belief that they will eventually get the opportunity to play the real game with the big boys on the field if they just stay active, loyal and supportive.

But, for all but a handful of the reps, success will never come their way. The owners, the coaches and the super-players were handpicked long before the team ever took the field. They were picked because they had already demonstrated the ability to win at various levels of the game prior to reaching the MLM majors.

And, thus, for the reps in the stands of the MLM Company, there is little chance they will ever be able to work their way up through the minor leagues to actually play on the money-making field. Their chances of getting to play in the Super Bowl game of an MLM are basically zero.

So, this brings us back to the questions that were asked at the start of this book. For what reasons are you thinking of joining an MLM? For fun? For the excitement of being with a lot of other enthusiastic fans? To learn the in's and out's of running your own business? To make a little spending money? To earn a decent living? Or to be wealthy beyond your wildest dreams?

If you are joining mostly for fun or to learn about running a business, go for it. As long as the expenses don't go beyond what you can comfortably afford, it doesn't matter if you make any money. That's not why you are joining.

If you are joining in hopes of making a decent living, just recognize that an MLM business is not that different from any other kind of business. To make a decent living will require hard work, long hours, and two-to-five years of consistent and persistent effort before you are likely to make a reasonable living.

If you are thinking of joining an MLM to become rich, you'd better possess nine or ten of the main characteristics that are the critical factors to having the opportunity to really succeed in an MLM business. If you aren't a natural born salesperson, and if you have not already demonstrated an ability to be successful in a real business, you would probably be better off buying lottery tickets as a way to have a chance to win a fortune.

But, as we all know, some little old lady in Peoria, Illinois, occasionally wins the big lottery. You can't win if you don't play. But, be realistic and recognize that there are only handful of lottery winners every year, and millions of losers.

Let me close with one other thought. I admit that I am not a big fan of MLM businesses. I personally believe they advertise false promises of wealth and untrue claims that <u>anyone</u> can make the big money. Unfortunately, these claims just aren't true. And what happens too often is that regular, honest, trusting people place a lot of hope and faith in these claims. They join an MLM business full of hope and energy and then they put their heart and soul into making it big.

When they don't, and 99% won't, they leave the business believing they are a failure. They leave thinking that they must be a terrible person and a worthless individual because they couldn't make it happen, even though the MLM Company promised that "*anyone can do this.*"

If you decide to get into an MLM business, or if you are already in one, and if you give it your best shot but can't make it work the way you hoped, please understand that you most likely didn't fail because you are a bad or incompetent person. The truth is, you entered into a game that you were never going to be properly equipped to play. It is unlikely that you had the characteristics, the experience, or the connections to become one of the real players.

Your chances of making it big in an MLM are no better than winning the lottery or getting to play in the Super Bowl. Have fun being a spectator if you want, but don't get down on yourself if you don't win. The game was loaded against you before the MLM ever opened its doors.

Hawkeye Richardson

About the Author

Hawkeye Richardson has been an author, speaker, and business consultant for over 30 years. He brings a unique, objective, outside-the-box perspective to business. He works with business owners and managers to help them find more effective, profitable, and enjoyable ways to operate their companies.

He presents his commonsense ideas in books, speeches and seminars to companies, organizations and associations. He also presents to groups of individuals who are interested in improving the effectiveness of their businesses and the quality of their lives.

He is the author of "*Getting Your 'It' Together -- Simple Suggestions for Attracting the Life You Want*", 2009, and "*How to Make Your Advertising More Effective*", 2007.

If you would like to have Hawkeye work with your organization or speak to your group, you may contact him at the address below, or email him through his website. If you would like to comment on this book or share stories of how it has helped you, you can write or send an email to:

Hawkeye Richardson
7925 N. Oracle Rd., PMB #176
Tucson, AZ 85704
Email/website: www.HawkeyeBook.com

www.ingramcontent.com/pod-product-compliance
Lightning Source LLC
Chambersburg PA
CBHW071426170526
45165CB00001B/413